EVANGELISM AS A LIFESTYLE

Jim Petersen

NAVPRESS
A MINISTRY OF THE NAVIGATORS
P.O. Box 6000, Colorado Springs, Colorado 80934

The Navigators is an international, evangelical Christian organization. Jesus Christ gave his followers the Great Commission to go and make disciples (Matthew 28:19). The aim of The Navigators is to help fulfill that commission by multiplying laborers for Christ in every nation.

NavPress is the publishing ministry of The Navigators. NavPress publications are tools to help Christians grow. Although publications alone cannot make disciples or change lives, they can help believers learn biblical discipleship, and apply what they learn to their lives and ministries.

Library of Congress Catalog Card Number 80-83874
ISBN: 0-89109-475-X
14753

Fifth printing, 1982

Scripture quotations are from the *New International Version,* © 1978 by the New York International Bible Society.

Printed in the United States of America

To
*My readers' neighbors
whom I have never met,
but hope to—in Glory.*

CONTENTS

AUTHOR

Jim Petersen is the Divisonal Director for The Navigators in Latin America.

He grew up in a Christian home in Minneapolis, Minnesota, and graduated from the University of Minnesota. He also studied at Northwestern Bible College and Bethel College.

When Jim was twenty-one, God became the most important influence in his life and Jim began a consuming search for a better personal knowledge of him. The following year he approached Ed Reis, a Navigator representative, for more personal help. Jim attributes acquiring the vision and the skills needed to match his personal desire to be used by God to Ed's influence in his life.

Jim served as an area representative in Minneapolis-St. Paul from 1958 to 1961. Following a brief assignment at the Navigator international headquarters in Colorado Springs, Colorado, Jim and his wife, Marge, moved to Brazil in 1963 to open the Navigator ministry there. Jim became the Latin American Navigators Divisonal Director in 1972.

He and his wife, Marge, and their four children, Michelle, Todd, Raquel, and Rochelle, live in Campinas, Brazil.

FOREWORD

Jim Petersen has written *Evangelism as a Lifestyle* out of years of in-depth Bible study and applicational experience in a cross-cultural setting. There's no question that he has the right to speak out clearly and emphatically on both the theory and the practice of Christian ministry. He has been in the trenches on the front line carrying out the Great Commission.

Jim has discovered that some evangelistic methods taught around the world are frequently both biblically questionable and culturally lacking. He rightfully questions quick and easy approaches to evangelism—a definite reflection of the New Testament's influence on his thinking. He also tackles the pragmatic aspects of building an in-depth, quality ministry. He advocates not only sharing the gospel, but helping Christians mature in Christ. A unique and creative approach to ''body-building'' permeates his philosophy. He has discovered that personal evangelism cannot be separated from the collective witness of a group of Christians, particularly in a culture that has few good churches.

Every Christian—whether in a church or a para-church organization—will discover a very challenging and thought-provoking message in this book. If we follow Jim Petersen's instructions as well as his example, we'll be building the church according to solid biblical guidelines that must always be culturally applied. May his influence touch us all!

Gene A. Getz
Pastor, Fellowship Bible Church,
and Director, Dallas Center
for Church Renewal
Dallas, Texas

ACKNOWLEDGMENTS

This book would not have been written without the stimulation of my Brazilian friends, especially Osvaldo Simoes, Mario Nitsche, and Aldo Berndt, whose probing questions continually drove me back to the Bible in search of satisfying answers. A fellow American missionary, Ken Lottis, also provided encouragement and stimulation. Finally, Jake Barnett and Monte Unger helped me organize, refine, and share the results of my Bible study and personal experiences in the dimensions of evangelism.

NEW INSIGHTS ON TRADITIONAL EVANGELISM

Evangelism bound by tradition

IN 1963 MY family traveled by ship from the United States to Brazil. The trip marked a new beginning. We expected that. We did not expect that the sixteen days aboard ship would, in themselves, mark the beginning of discoveries that are still going on. This book is an attempt to pass on what I have been learning about evangelism since that trip.

There were 120 people on the ship. Half were tourists, and half were missionaries—including us. Sixty missionaries and sixty tourists! A one-to-one ratio for sixteen days. Since there isn't much more to do aboard ship other than walk, read, or converse, I couldn't imagine how any of those tourists could get through the trip without receiving a thorough exposure to the Christian message. More ideal conditions for evangelism couldn't exist.

During the first three days my wife and I spent our time relating to the other passengers. Conversations were unhurried and soon we found ourselves deeply involved in discussing Christ with our new acquaintances.

On the third day I thought that if the other fifty-eight missionaries were doing what we were, we would have a serious case of overkill. I decided to check with the others about coordinating our efforts. My first opportunity came when I encountered six missionaries sitting together on the deck. I joined them and expressed my concern, suggesting we get our signals straight so we wouldn't overwhelm the passengers.

I had totally misjudged the problem. When I explained what was on my mind, the six just looked at one another. Apparently, it hadn't occurred to them to talk to the other sixty passengers about Christ. Finally one said, "We just graduated from seminary and didn't learn how to do that sort of thing there." Another said, "I don't know. I have sort of a built-in reservation against the idea of conversion." A third said, "I've been a pastor for three years, but I've never personally evangelized anyone. I don't think I know how either."

I remember saying that if we, in sixteen days and with a one-to-one ratio, couldn't evangelize sixty people, we might as well forget about ninety-five million Brazilians. Perhaps it would be just as well if we would all catch the next boat north.

A few hours later there was a knock on our cabin door. I opened it to find three of the six I had just been talking to. They had come to tell me they had obtained permission from the captain to conduct a Sunday service for the ship's crew and that they wanted me to preach the sermon.

As they elaborated their plan, I was reminded of a conversation I had three weeks before with a friend's pastor. The pastor told me his congregation had recently begun witnessing. He said the young people were going to the old folks' home each Sunday to conduct a service. Some of his men were holding weekly jail services after which they would counsel prisoners individually.

Obviously, there is nothing wrong with conducting services in jails and rest homes, but if such things alone constitute the main evangelistic thrust of a body of Christians it raises a problem. I asked the pastor, "Aren't you running the risk of teaching your congregation that the gospel is only for those in unfortunate circumstances—for those who are relatively unthreatening to us? Shouldn't Christians learn to carry the message to their peers, to go after people on their own level?"

I expressed the same concern to the three missionaries in my cabin. We could slip into the same mental trap aboard ship. I said, "Your consciences were pricked by what we talked about. So now you've spotted the unfortunate sailors who never go to church and have planned a service for them. That is good, but I don't think we can escape from our responsibility to the passengers."

They got the point, but they had already committed themselves to conducting a service for the crew. The captain posted a notice in the crew's quarters, and arrangements had been made to use the galley. I agreed to attend, but not to speak.

The four of us arrived in the galley on schedule. It was empty. Occasionally a sailor would have to go through the room in the course of his duties. He would dart through quickly, obviously intent on not getting caught. Finally, one sailor came in and sat down. He was a Baptist. So we had the service: four missionaries and one Baptist sailor!

After that, my three friends began to think in terms of going to the tourists.

There was an elderly Christian couple among the passengers. It was the husband's birthday so the three missionaries organized an old-fashioned sing to commemorate the occasion. Sensing what was coming and not wanting to jeopardize my relationships with the people I was evangelizing, I felt it wiser to stay away. When the time came for the program, I was up on the third deck. One other passenger was up there enjoying the night air. We began discussing the New Testament I had taken along to read.

Down below we could hear the old songs: "Swannee River," "My Old Kentucky Home"; then it was "Rock of

Ages", another hymn, a pause. And so it went: hymns, testimonies, and a message.

When it was over my three friends were euphoric. They had succeeded in "preaching" to virtually all the passengers. Naturally, they called another sing for two nights later. Once again I went to the third deck, but this time there were sixty others up there with me. They weren't about to get caught twice!

As I later reflected on those sixteen days aboard ship, it occurred to me that this situation represented a microcosm of the church in the world. That realization, combined with the subsequent years of adapting to a new culture and language for the sake of the gospel, has raised scores of questions and set me on a quest that continues to this day. This search has to do with what it really means to take the gospel into the world—the subject of this book.

========================ONE========================

FACING REALITY: THE UNREACHED WORLD

Are we moving in the right direction?

"GO INTO ALL the world" (Mark 16:15). How do you visualize the world when you read these words of Jesus?

One way is to see it as a sphere inhabited by more than four billion individuals, among whom the only important distinction is their relationship to God through Jesus Christ. The task is huge, but simple: Get the gospel message to all who don't know Christ.

Or you can think geographically. There are about 165 independent countries in the world today. We need to cross national borders and establish our work and witness in as many of these countries as possible. How often we measure our success in the missionary enterprise by counting the number of countries in which we are involved! The task of world evangelization is then oversimplifed to establishing the same organization using the same methods in more countries of the world.

15

Instead, we should think in terms of *people*. The Missions Advanced Research and Communication Center (MARC) of World Vision, Incorporated, presented a report entitled *Unreached Peoples Directory* to the International Congress on World Evangelism in Lausanne, Switzerland, in 1974.

> God in Christ obligated all Christians to the evangelization, not of the countries of the world, but of the *ta ethne*, the *peoples* of the world.[1]
>
> Sin deep in our hearts has blinded us to the wonderful truth that God not only loves all the peoples of the world, but he loves them *to be different from each other*, just as a gardner rejoices in all the different brilliant colors and designs of the flowers that God has created for his garden.[2]
>
> We see the concept of *peoples* to be absolutely basic to the evangelistic perspective of the apostle Paul. . . . He worked as a Jew, with all due respect to Jewish cultural tradition. . . . He respected the Greek way of life, so long as it was submitted to Jesus Christ as Lord in the most profound Biblical and spiritual sense.[3]
>
> Evangelization must take seriously the hues and colors, the contours and the character of the diverse peoples of the world.[4]
>
> Many missionaries have confused the fact that God loves all peoples, both high and low, with a false ideal of eliminating all differences. . . . Fortunately, there is a rising appreciation for the many different and amazingly complex languages and cultures around the world. Proper evangelistic sensitivity to the concept of peoples is of immense importance.[5]

Dr. Charles R. Taber, editor of *Practical Anthropology* and translations consultant for the United Bible Societies, is also quoted: "Because societies, cultures, and individuals vary so much, the most effective evangelistic approach is the one which is most specifically geared to the particular situation of the hearer. The evangelist . . . must discover what assumptions the hearer holds about reality, truth, and value."

This emphasis on appropriate strategies in modern missions is highly encouraging. Biblical strategies which take into account the ethnic distinctions, cultural differences, and "assumptions the hearer holds about reality, truth, and value" are essential. A World Vision executive said, "MARC correctly recognized that no major inroads would be made on behalf of the gospel unless there was a well-defined strategy to reach the unreached. This strategy, they concluded, must be people-centered rather than evangelist-centered."

All of these observations are concerned with the process of communicating the gospel—in Taber's words, to "maximize the fit of the gospel presentation to the hearer's needs." In these quoted studies, the primary purpose of understanding "peoples" and their culture is to enable the proper adaptation of the *verbal proclamation* of the gospel message.

This book suggests a biblically-based strategy for evangelism, but I am convinced that we need to go one step further than proclamation to discover an effective strategy based on Scripture. We need to recognize that the proclamation of the gospel was only the first step in Paul's strategy. Something more dynamic than proclamation alone is needed to reach *unreached peoples*.

Eight hundred million people live today in countries that are nominally Christian, a term that is nearly synonymous with Western civilization. MARC places the other 3.2 billion in seven categories: animist, Buddhist, Christo-pagan, Hindu, Islamic, traditional tribal beliefs, and secularist.

The inclusion of the "secularist" especially interests me. This book's subject is reaching the unreached with the gospel. My experience has been in the United States and the developed portions of Brazil. The major unreached group in both areas *is* the secularized. This is a book about reaching the secularized with the gospel, but to some degree we are using the word in a new way, so a careful definition is necessary.

Secular is defined as "pertaining to worldly things, or to things that are not regarded as religious, spiritual, or sacred." *Secularized* is "made secular, separate from religions or spiritual connection or influences, made worldly or unspiritual.'' The first definition reflects simply a nonreligious existence; the second implies that there has been a transformation *from* a religious life to a nonreligious existence.

We can combine these definitions to describe a large segment of the world's population: "people not operating within a religious framework.'' Religion is not a vital aspect of their existence. Their personal philosophy of life is not based on religious concepts.

This description would include the purely "secular"— those with a totally nonreligious philosophy. It would also include the atheist, the agnostic, and those whose materialistic philosophy has become for them a quasi-religion, as it is for the Marxist.

It would also include those who have "become" secularized, who have made a transition from a religious philosophy to a nonreligious one. A few may have made this transition within their own lifetime. More often the transition involves several generations of disillusionment with religion. Many of these people are at least a generation removed from experiencing life within a religious framework. They feel that religion has been exhausted as a valid basis for a personal philosophy. They are postreligious.

They may have a traditional knowledge of religion, but no personal religious life. Some in this category may even have an extensive knowledge of religious concepts. As an example, the catechism may have been part of their education. If asked about religion they will give the "right" answers. But they do not attribute any validity to those religious concepts.

Others are totally ignorant of religious matters, even of the existence of religion. It may be difficult for most of us to imagine this, but there are population segments even in the United States where this is true.

There are, of course, degrees of secularization. The extremes on any continuum are easy to identify, but often the distinctions are not that absolute. Between black and white lie an infinite number of shades of gray. Many individuals are partially secularized and partially religious.

How much of the American population could be considered secularized? The *Christianity Today*-Gallup Poll of Americans over eighteen in 1979 found that 94 percent of Americans believed in God or in a universal spirit who functions in their minds as God. One-half of these said this belief gave them great comfort. About one-fourth believed that Jesus is fully God and fully man. Forty-five percent said personal faith in Christ is the only hope of heaven.

Church membership in the United States is now 67 percent. Half of the members attend church at least monthly. This includes Protestants, Catholics, and other denominations. One in five adult Americans identify themselves as evangelicals.[6]

How do we interpret these survey results? Obviously they reflect a wide dissemination of the gospel message. But what about the half of that 94 percent who find little or no comfort in the God they believe in? Apparently their position is a simple deism—a belief in a God who perhaps created the world and then withdrew—rather than thinking of him as one who is actively involved in the affairs of men.

In the MARC report quoted earlier, Dr. Taber asks, "What populations are today's unreached?" Taber explains: "These are not only small, whole, homogeneous populations, such as remote jungle tribes and bands, but definable sub-populations within otherwise well evangelized societies, or groups which were evangelized in a previous century or generation but not in this. This includes a great many churchgoers in the prosperous suburbs of Western countries for example, who for all their churchianity have never come to grips with a clear presentation of the Gospel. . . . It can well be said that for all practical purposes, these people are just as unreached as the jungle tribes or as the masses of urban ghettos."

The theologian Reinhold Niebuhr warned us to "take no satisfaction in the prevailing religiosity of our nation. Much of it is a perversion of the Christian gospel."[7]

I would like to make an intuitive judgment: In view of such statistics, my own experience, and our definition of the word *secular* is it not reasonable to regard half of the American population as secularized—as people not operating within a religious framework?

My missionary experience has been among secularized people. I also serve with a Christian organization that ministers throughout the world. My associates who are ministering to other unreached peoples are learning some of the same lessons I am learning. I believe the same principles apply wherever we cross the frontiers of our own subculture and attempt to bring the good news to people who do not share our presuppositions, and who have not been previously prepared to respond to a proclamation of the gospel. We are not doing well in crossing these cultural frontiers. We are, in fact, talking to ourselves!

The gospel is the power of God for salvation—present and future. It is basic to resolving any human need, whether individual or collective. It is the good news that God has by his grace provided for the reconciliation of all that has been marred by the fall (see Romans 8:19-32).

If this is true, its communication deserves our most diligent study and pursuit. There can be no more critical issue. One of the primary hindrances to a greater effectiveness in communicating the gospel is the prevailing attitude that we basically have the answers to how to win the lost when, in fact, we do not. We seem to feel we know what evangelism is all about, and that now it's just a matter of time, manpower, and money before the job will be accomplished. We have ceased to search for more effective approaches.

One of the benefits of my attempts to take the gospel across cultural and linguistic frontiers is that in the course of the journey my best and most unassailable ideas were destroyed. Few of my methods survived the transition, and those that did probably shouldn't have. Stripped, I discovered my ignorance, which lay buried all along. This was an extremely valuable experience, for awakening to one's ignorance is the dawn of learning.

Over the past eighteen years I have considered many

questions relating to the mobility of the gospel. Many remain unanswered (including some of those I will list), but I have learned enough to realize I have sometimes been oblivious to some major biblical truths. Consequently, these have been years of searching. My desire is to enlist you in this search, so together we may contribute to the progress of the gospel in the world.

Here are some of the questions I've faced:

What about the world we live in? How accurate is our perception of it? Do we understand what is really going on in the minds of those around us? Are we aware of where modern man's philosophy has taken him? Do we know where he is emotionally?

What about secularization? Do we know the extent to which the world around us has become secularized? How do we communicate with the secularized? Is it even possible?

What is genuine communication? To what degree do we have to consider differences in mentality when we share Christ? When can we know the gospel has been communicated? When we fail to communicate, who is responsible? Just how do we adapt to our hearers?

What did Jesus mean when he said the gospel is to be preached to "every creature" and in "all the world"? At what point have we fulfilled this command? Is it when we have proclaimed the terms of the contract to someone, or is there more to it than that? Are evangelism and "reaping" synonymous?

What did Jesus mean when he told us we are to be "in the world"? How do we reconcile this with "coming out from among them"? What is the balance between involvement with the world and isolation? Are we in the world as Jesus intended or are we ghettoized?

What about the great things that are happening in the church today; the big crusades, the seminars, the super churches? Given time and adequate manpower will they not accomplish the commands of Christ? Will our programs and institutions fill the need? If not, what's missing?

Who is responsible for the advance of the gospel in the

world? Is it realistic to expect every Christian to be involved? Or are we loading our brothers with false guilt? What about personal evangelism? Is that the answer? Where does the church fit into the picture? Is personal evangelism only for the gifted few?

As I searched for answers I realized that the Christian mission is far more complex and varied than we are willing to admit. Our limited success in communicating across the frontiers of different mentalities and cultures convinced me that we must be overlooking some major scriptural truths in this matter of communicating the gospel to the world. We have so reduced our understanding of evangelism that we are left surrounded by a secularized world, a world we are so accustomed to that we are scarcely aware it exists. We are not effectively communicating with secularized men and women.

This may be true now, but it doesn't have to remain that way. It is possible to effectively communicate the gospel to all kinds of people. But to do so we must first expand our understanding of what the Scriptures teach about evangelism. That is the purpose of this book: to awaken our awareness to the world of people around us and to call our attention to some biblical truths we have been neglecting. We will be developing the concept that there are two primary modes of evangelism in the Scriptures. They are:

1. The *proclamation* of the gospel: an *action* through which the non-Christian receives a clear statement of the essential message.
2. The *affirmation* of the gospel: a *process* of modeling and explaining the Christian message.

We will find that both of these modes are essential if we are to reach all kinds. But both are also limited. We are more familiar with the first, often treating it as the comprehensive means of evangelism, while, in fact, it is intended as an initial phase. In the past we have focused on proclamation and almost ignored affirmation.

Much more of our society is reachable than we imagine— although these people may not be immediately reapable. It is time to believe God for a larger slice of the dominion of darkness than we are getting. It can be done, but it will demand change.

Footnotes:

1. *Unreached Peoples Directory* (Monrovia, California: Missions Advanced Research and Communications Center, 1974), page 12.
2. Ibid., page 9
3. Ibid., page 10
4. Ibid.
5. Ibid., page 11
6. "The Christianity Today-Gallup Poll: An Overview," *Christianity Today* Vol. XXIII (December 21, 1979), page 12.
7. Reinhold Niebuhr, "Religiosity and the Christian Faith," *Christianity in Crisis* (May 28, 1951), reprinted in *Reinhold Niebuhr Essays in Applied Christianity*, ed. D.B. Robertson (New York: Meridian, Living Age, 1959), page 65.

TWO

A RUDE AWAKENING
Are we patient enough?

OSVALDO WAS AMONG the first Brazilians I talked to about Christ. The experience was unforgettable. He was working as an industrial chemist when I looked him up. We knew each other through his brother, with whom I was studying the Scriptures. Osvaldo was curious about what was going on because he couldn't imagine his brother becoming involved in anything religious. His brother just wasn't that kind of person. So, when I invited Osvaldo to dinner in our home, he eagerly accepted.

The conversation began with Osvaldo asking questions about our motives for being in Brazil and about what was happening between his brother and me. The best way I could think to answer his questions was to explain the gospel to him. I got a piece of chalk and a Bible and used the wooden floor as a chalkboard. I spent the next two hours showing him a favorite diagram I often used to explain the message. I was quite satisfied with my performance, and when I finally finished, I leaned back to observe his reaction, certain he would be on the verge of repentance.

Instead, he gazed at my illustration, then at me. He was puzzled. "Do you mean to tell me that this is why you came all the way to Brazil, to tell people that?" he said.

To Osvaldo, what I had said seemed insignificant and irrelevant. I recognized at that moment that I was facing a communication problem I had never been aware of before. In my mind I had always equated evangelism with reaping. But here before me was an empty field. Planting, watering, and cultivation would have to occur before I could hope to reap.

I invited Osvaldo to begin reading the Scriptures with me. For the next three months we met several times a week to read and discuss the Gospel of John together. His movement from a free-thinker's humanistic philosophy towards accepting the truth of Christ was plainly visible and the process resulted in his submission to Christ.

The method of using such a sustained exposure to the Scriptures became a pattern. I soon found I was bringing people to Christ in Brazil that I would have passed up as indifferent or out of reach in the United States. I also found that these new Christians, born after a longer period of gestation, had fewer spiritual problems. Spiritual casualties were rare. "Good soil . . . produced a crop, multiplying thirty, sixty, or even a hundred times" (Mark 4:8).

I had expanded my understanding of evangelism to include planting, watering, and cultivating as well as reaping. I learned that evangelism is a process.

When we bring someone to a decision to trust in Christ in the course of a conversation or two, we can be sure of one thing: Considerable preparation and laboring has already occurred in that life before we arrived on the scene. I think this is what Jesus was saying to the twelve in John 4:36-38: "The reaper draws his wages, even now he harvests the crop for eternal life, so that the sower and the reaper may be glad together. Thus the saying, 'One sows and another reaps' is true. I sent you to reap what you have not worked for. Others have done the hard work, and you have reaped the benefits of their labor.''

God uses many influences to accomplish the necessary preparation: people, circumstances, and events.

Some of the essential steps along the way only he alone can accomplish. The God-consciousness planted in the heart of every man is one of these (see Romans 1:20). God has also written his law in men's hearts, accompanying it with a conscience and sense of guilt (see Romans 2:14-15).

Sometimes he uses political situations. Josiah found a dusty copy of the Scriptures in the temple and led his nation to revival. Economic uncertainties, political upheavals, revolutions that disrupt the routines and values of normal life—all of these events can serve to draw people along the continuum away from the dominion of darkness and toward the kingdom of light.

Even chance comments can be significant. An ex-Buddhist friend, describing his conversion to Christ, pointed back to a comment by his mother while they were in the Buddhist temple as being the trigger that started his search that led him to Christ. She wondered aloud why the "true God" was positioned last, not first, on the shelf of idols in the temple. He never forgot his mother's question. Her comment prepared him to respond to the Christian gospel.

God uses an endless variety of ways and means to sow the seed of the gospel message and move us along from ignorance and rebellion toward faith. The most obvious means, and by far the most effective, is a strong Christian family— growing up where the fundamentals of Christianity are practiced and taught in the home and church. After such an education, often the sole remaining need is reaping. People with a Christian heritage still exist in significant number in many places. In those situations, reaping by itself produces encouraging results. But this can mislead us into thinking the whole world is at the same level of preparedness. It can make us forget that evangelism is, in fact, a process.

This was my experience, at least. My own first efforts at influencing people for Christ reflected this misconception. As a young Christian I had acquired the habit of spending considerable amounts of time studying and meditating on the Scriptures. The positive effects this had on me were obvious, and I was excited about what was happening to me. But I also grew restless because I knew witnessing was expected of any Christian who was serious about following Christ. The thought of witnessing paralyzed me with fear, however, and I couldn't bring myself to open my mouth.

I had a mental caricature of what a "good witness" was like. In part this image was derived from my concept of the apostle Paul: preaching to the philosophers on Mars Hill, speaking in the market place, or conversing with the praetorian guard. Projected into contemporary society, I imagined a good witness was like a good salesman—unabashed, aggressive, fearless of strangers. But my world was full of strangers, and I was afraid of them. I concluded I didn't "have the gift" and tried to put evangelism out of my mind.

That didn't work either. Inner tension continued to build. I *wanted* to evangelize. On several occasions I would drop whatever I was doing, get into my car and drive to the Student Union at the University of Minnesota where I was studying, determined to witness to someone. I made several clandestine trips, but never talked to a soul. Finally, I revealed my frustrations to a mature Christian who I knew was a fruitful witness. In response, he took me with him to a university campus where I watched him spend the afternoon initiating conversations that led into opportunities to present the gospel. Terror gave way to enthusiasm as I discovered personal witnessing wasn't impossible. The experience was a breakthrough.

Over the next months I witnessed to all of my friends. Some became Christians, others did not. As I pressed each person to decide, my relationships with those who refused became strained. Soon I had polarized all my friendships. But that was fine with me because I had overcome my frustration. I even thought the polarization reflected my spiritual integrity!

With no friends left to witness to, I began to visit student dormitories, going from door to door. I tried fraternity meetings and visited military bases. Some people became Christians as a result of my efforts, but the casualty rate was almost as high as the birth rate. I simply explained away my poor results with the parable of the sower: Poor soil—it was their fault, not mine. It was with this mistaken mentality that I found myself in Brazil talking to Osvaldo.

THREE

THE REAPING MENTALITY

Are we too anxious for the harvest?

SEVERAL YEARS AGO a close friend visited us in Curitiba, Brazil. He was a missionary with ten years' experience in organizing citywide evangelistic crusades. He and his team would enter a city, unite the pastors, and spend three to six months training counselors, organizing follow-up, and making other necessary preparations.

We were sitting in his Volkswagen bus, parked in front of the post office, when he said, "I'm going to try it one more time. I've been at this for ten years and I've yet to see any permanent results for my efforts. We organize a crusade and there are scores of decisions. Local pastors give glowing testimonials to the effect that their churches have been transformed. But then it's all over. When we return three months later there is not a trace to show we were there at all. If things aren't different after this next attempt, I'm going to give up, return to the United States, and go into business."

And that's what he did! Such frustration and disillusionment are the fruits of attempting to reap where there has been little previous labor. Let me give some examples of the limitations of the reaping approach to evangelism.

The idea of "saturation evangelism" was born some years ago. In his book *Frontiers In Missionary Strategy,* Peter Wagner writes that the aim of this form of evangelism was "to present the gospel in spoken and written form to every people of the land, to every stratum of society, to every home and individual. . . . Saturation evangelism seeks to mobilize and train every believer available to become an active and effective evangelizer for Christ."[1]

These are stirring objectives. I could easily give my life to seeing them accomplished—if only they were realistic!

Saturation evangelism crusades have been carried out on numerous occasions in Latin America and in other countries. But studies done on their effectiveness by various missiologists show little or no lasting growth. Wagner quotes Dr. George Peters of Dallas Theological Seminary who concluded, "from the records and statistics available there is no appreciable, immediate, and measurable acceleration in church growth evident in most churches . . . in the years following the campaigns."

In fact, Wagner shows that the church was actually growing better *before* the "in-depth" effort. Citing an example in Bolivia, he says, "The percentage of annual growth of the seven cooperating denominations . . . was greater during the year just before Evangelism in Depth than it was either during the year of effort or during the two following years."[2]

In country after country, mobilization has successfully occurred during the Evangelism in Depth year, but at the end of the effort it has fallen off. Why is this? "For one thing," Wagner explains, "the majority of people who participate suffer from sheer exhaustion. The pressure of the program saps the energy from all involved. Some discontinue their regular activities . . . and afterwards they find themselves with a huge backlog of work. Some postpone their vacations and then feel that they deserve a double one. . . . Some leaders came out with a bad case of . . . 'evangelistic indigestion,' from which it took them a full year to recover."[3]

Dr. Win Arn, President of the Institute for American Church Growth, examined several sets of results from a recent large-scale evangelistic campaign in an article in *Church Growth: America* magazine.

A typical set of results noted: 140 leaders trained; 7,200 telephone calls made; material shared with 1,987; 525 decisions; 72 interested enough to enroll in Bible study (with 20 of these becoming new church members, of which 16 had previous church affiliation).[4]

The results were from a North American, Midwest "Bible-belt" city. I would expect even lesser results in areas with fewer prepared people. Of course church membership is not the exclusive measurement for evaluating results and I do not question the validity of the efforts—results were produced.

These kinds of evangelistic programs are gigantic efforts, requiring overwhelming organization—but they produced disappointing results! This will be the predictable outcome wherever we try to maintain a reaping mentality while evangelizing among unprepared peoples.

The overall evangelistic thrust of most local churches is producing disappointing results as far as reaching out to the secularized. One very successful church in Minneapolis recently employed a marketing analysis firm to do research among the 200,000 people within ten-minutes drive of the church. Eighty-six percent were totally unaware of the church's existence, even though it is quite prominent and located on a main thoroughfare. Only seven percent thought there was any possibility they would ever visit the church.

Another Minneapolis pastor shared these results of his six-year ministry in an evangelical church of 350 members: Of 159 new members during this time, 117 came by transfer from other churches. Thirty-six were children of church members, leaving 6 that could have been converts.

The same problem is also observable in much of the

evangelism conducted on a smaller scale and even on the individual level. I could fill this book with accounts of my own efforts and those of others I've observed where reliance on proclamation produced meager, temporary results.

I do not intend this as criticism. We should give thanks whenever the gospel is communicated in any form. The point is that we must change our tactics if we hope to effectively evangelize the unreached segments of our population.

RESTRICTING COMMUNICATION

Dr. Ralph Winter, Director of the United States Center for World Mission, has observed, "Nominal Christians emerge automatically in the second generation and seem everywhere eventually to ring the Christian church around like a soft doughnut, which then in turn prevents the committed Christians from even getting out beyond that doughnut to the non-Christian world."[5] In other words, he asserts that we are exhausting our evangelistic energies on ourselves—on the nominal Christians who surround us. Can this be so?

Several years ago I became suspicious about the effectiveness of our communication with the secularized. I tried to answer the question, Just who are we reaching in our evangelistic efforts? I soon discovered that information such as this is hard to find. For one thing, we are not accustomed to thinking in these categories. For another, it is difficult to find accurate data on the state of Christianity in the United States. So I devised a simple test that would at least reveal how my circle of colaborers were faring in this area.

I have estimated that up to half of the American population does not view Christianity as the basis for their personal philosophy. They might, if pressed for religious preference, opt for Christianity, but for practical purposes it is meaningless. It seemed to me that if we were effectively reaching the unreached half of our population, those converts would have to show up somewhere in the body of Christ. So I formulated a question and have posed it to Christian audiences at every opportunity for several years.

I have asked this question in churches, seminaries, conferences, and in university campus groups. I have been especially interested in the campus groups because these are usually "grassroots" situations. My own organization, The Navigators, holds to a philosophy of "growing our own disciples" by evangelizing the lost and training converts in discipleship. Consequently, the starting point for any local Navigator ministry is evangelism. For obvious reasons, I would be anxious to survey such gatherings because they usually include many new Christians won through personal evangelism. I wanted to discover where they came from. Did they have a church background, or were they from the world? Were any of them won to Christ in a secularized context?

The question I ask is: "How many of you do not have a Christian heritage? That is, how many of you did not attend church with some regularity at some point in your youth?"

My rationale: Their responses would quickly divide the audience into two categories, the religious and the secularized. By comparing this response against my estimate of the national profile (half the population is secularized, half has a religious heritage), we would arrive at some notion as to our effectiveness among the secularized.

With a few notable exceptions, I discovered that roughly 90 percent of those in our Christian structures have a religious heritage. Rarely have I found a group where more than one in ten came from a secularized background. In other words, approximately 90 percent of the active Christians on campuses have come from that half of the population that has had extensive previous religious exposure, while only about 10 percent comes from the secularized half.

EVANGELISTIC CRUSADES

A few years ago I had the opportunity to discuss this subject with Charlie Riggs of the Billy Graham Team. Mr. Riggs has been with the Graham team for more than twenty years and has been responsible for follow-up for most of that time.

I asked him what kind of people were coming to Christ

through the Graham Crusades twenty years ago—where did they come from? Then I asked where the people were coming from who are responding today. He explained that in the early years those making decisions were generally from the "liberal churches where they were not hearing the gospel." But now, he said, more than 90 percent of those making decisions are from "our evangelical churches."

I asked him when this transition occurred and how he interpreted it. He replied that the shift took place in the middle 1960s. He thinks "the tree has been shaken." In other words, the bulk of the unreached who would respond to a proclamation of the gospel have done so!

The accomplishment of reaching those who have responded to the gospel cannot be minimized. But we cannot allow ourselves to think the gospel has been completely communicated—even in North America. Communication implies a minimum of two: a teller and a listener. People are highly selective in what they hear and pay attention to. Therefore, those of us who communicate the gospel must improve the ways we communicate.

DEDUCTIONS

I readily admit my approach is anything but scientific, and that my conclusions are subject to many exceptions. But I will have to leave a precise study for someone more disposed to pursuing this kind of research. Since my figures are more impressionistic than precise, you may want to test them yourself as they relate to your situation. It should be a simple thing to do. Simply compare the religious profile of your city or suburb against that of your own local fellowship. How does your fellowship rate in reaching the secularized?

What does all of this tell us? If 90 percent of our fruit is coming from the half of the population who have at some point already been among us, we have a communication problem with the other half. It means we have yet to cross the frontiers of different mentalities and reach those from non-Christian, secular backgrounds with the gospel.

We cannot deceive ourselves into thinking we are already effectively discharging our trust to share the gospel. Nor can we think that if we keep doing what we have been doing—and even redouble our efforts—we are going to reach our world. It will take more than that. Our patterns of evangelism must change.

As the Billy Graham Association was making preparations for a Congress On Evangelism in the early 1970s, they issued a statement summarizing the intended thrust of the Congress. *Church Growth Bulletin* published the statement under the title: "Billy Graham's New Vision."[6] The article noted plans were being made that

> will, for the first time, tackle a startling problem, formerly overlooked: most (at least one billion) of the unreached peoples of the world are not within the normal evangelistic range of any church anywhere. This fact is surprising since we know that there are now Christian churches in every country of the world. The problem is that ordinary evangelistic efforts simply do not carry effectively across the high barriers constituted by ethnic, cultural, and social differences. It is an embarrassing fact that the churches in the United States and around the world, which are geographically closest to these unevangelized peoples, or ethnic groups, are often the farthest away from them culturally and emotionally. . . . This amazing new element smashed the illusion many Christians have had that the world can be won if only the worldwide Church will evangelize the people with whom it is normally in contact.

For me, the most disturbing thing in connection with this statement is the amazement of the reporter!

CONCLUSION

Our limited ability to communicate also has a direct bearing on the effectiveness of our world missions. In a recent worldwide survey of one Christian mission organization working in more than thirty countries, it was discovered that eighty-seven percent of the people it had reached already had a Protestant heritage!

Perhaps we are going to have to learn to communicate effectively with the secularized within our own culture in order to be truly effective outside of it. Are we sending people who are limited to working only among those who share our own evangelical presuppositions?

Where are the apostles to the Gentiles in this generation?

Footnotes:

1. C. Peter Wagner, *Frontiers in Missionary Strategy* (Chicago: Moody Press, 1971), page 135.
2. Ibid., page 143.
3. Ibid., pages 159-160.
4. Win Arn, "A Church Growth Look at 'Here's Life America,'" *Church Growth: America*, (January-February 1977), page 7.
5. Ralph Winter, "Who Are the Three Billion? Part II," *Church Growth Bulletin* (July, 1977), pages 139-144.
6. "Billy Graham's New Vision," *Church Growth Bulletin* (November, 1972), page 278.

FOUR

REAL COMMUNICATION
Does our audience understand us?

IN THE MIDDLE 1970s, three North American couples joined together as a team and moved to Caracas, Venezuela, to work as missonaries. All three couples were experienced, having spent several years in grassroots evangelism and discipling on university campuses and in communities.

Their initial target in Caracas was the university student. They spent their days on the campuses, explaining the gospel to anyone who would listen, initiating relationships, conducting Bible studies, and attempting by every possible means to establish a nucleus of new Christians who would eventually join them in their efforts.

In several ways, Caracas is unique. It is oil rich, and public works abound. The currency is strong and jobs are relatively plentiful. Job seekers have flowed there from Europe and North as well as South America. Money comes easily to everyone but the poor. The city has become a crowded cosmopolis with nowhere left to grow, since it is wedged among the Andes Mountains. Historically, Caracas has resisted the Christianizing attempts of both the Roman Catholic and Protestant churches. What this all adds up to is a basically pagan society with little else but materialism to live for.

After a full year of hard work with very little fruit, one of the missionaries wrote me: "We all agree we are learning to do evangelism all over again. Or perhaps it's that we're learning to truly evangelize for the first time. In the States, more often than not, when doing cold evangelism, a person's head will drop as soon as you mention God, the Bible, or spiritual things. That never happens here! More often than not, their response is more like, 'What a pity!'" In other words, the Caracas students were sorry to see these otherwise normal people involved in such folly.

The letter continued, "We don't see much evidence of conviction of sin nor of any sense of need. . . . There is absolutely no interest in the Bible or in what it has to say."

What was happening? Why were those couples not seeing the same response in Caracas that they would in a typical American city? Two variables, the audience and the communicators, were worlds apart. Remember this problem is not one just missionaries face. The same difficulty will be faced by individuals sharing the gospel anywhere.

1. THE AUDIENCE

There is a significant difference between the spiritual heritage of the average non-Christian in Caracas and the average North American who is not a Christian. Not all the people in the world are equally predisposed to respond to the gospel.

Paul made some fascinating observations about this in his Mars Hill discourse. He declared it was God's idea to compartmentalize the world into races, languages, cultures, and nations.

Paul said, "He himself gives men life and breath and everything else. From one man he made every nation of men, that they should inhabit the whole earth; and he determined the times [periods of history] set for them and the exact places [geographical locations] where they should live. God did this so that men would seek him and find him, though he is not far from each one of us'' (Acts 17:25-27).

Having spent a good part of my life struggling with cultural and linguistic barriers, I tended to view them as something this world could easily do without. So it was a surprise to discover that the existing arrangement was God's idea and that he did it this way with the reconciliation of the world in mind! Apparently, these barriers serve as a preservative, limiting the influence of the decadent or burned-out cultures on the others (see Genesis 11:1-9).

For this discussion the important thing to recognize is that not every nation or people is at the same point of preparedness. This is certainly going to affect the kind of communication that must take place and the degree of response one receives as one moves from a typical American city to a foreign and secularized one like Caracas.

This comes into focus quite easily when we compare a Bible-belt city in America with an unreached city like Caracas. Yet it is just as true, but perhaps more obscure, that similar distances exist between Christians and non-Christians even within our American cities!

2. THE COMMUNICATORS

What happens when a communicator attempts to carry on a conversation with someone who does not share the same presuppositions or the same emotional conditionings?

Recently, I observed a conversation between a young missionary and a non-Christian Latin American student. The missionary was experiencing the excruciating frustration of unwittingly turning his non-Christian acquaintances away every time he attempted to discuss the gospel with them.

On this occasion he had made an appointment with a friend with whom he had played soccer for several months. Hoping that an observer could help him understand what was going wrong, the missionary invited me along.

He began well. He explained that the purpose for his moving to that country was his involvement in a Christian student movement. He was there with the intent of finding people who were interested in examining the Scriptures to see if they held the answers for life's questions. Then he went on to explain that in order for him to do this effectively, he first needed to understand the mentality of those he was trying to influence. So far, so good.

He then proceeded to ask certain questions of his friend. These, too, were well-received, but he soon ran into difficulty.

The questions ranged over the basic Christian beliefs: What was his concept of God? Who was Jesus Christ? What was his concept of salvation? All these his friend answered readily, with answers straight out of the catechism!

Accepting these answers at face value, my friend assumed he was dealing with a person who shared many of his own presuppositions. This was his first mistake. His second soon followed.

The student asked my friend how he would answer those same questions. He probably shouldn't have answered at all at this point, but he mistook the question as an opportunity and seized it. His reply was, in his own eyes, a clear synthesis of the Christian message. Jesus was God. He died for our sins. We can be reconciled to God by grace through faith, and so on.

I watched the student as my friend talked. Disappointment was written on his face. He did not really accept the catechism he had just quoted. In fact, he had long since given up on religion. His answers had been a trial balloon. He liked this American and hoped that what he had to offer would somehow be different. But the differences between his catechism and what he was hearing from the American were too subtle for the student to grasp. Both the speaker and the listener were unwittingly communicating in separate languages. They used identical terminology, but never realized that the message each received and the ways they interpreted the meanings of the words they used differed greatly.

The student interpreted what was said as a reinforcement of his rejected religion.

My missionary friend had unknowingly, but irreversibly, pigeonholed himself! Instead of sharing his beliefs immediately, he should have asked additional questions until he was sure he understood what his friend thought and believed. He should have spoken only when his friend was truly ready to listen.

When people differ in their starting points, as these two did, this is often the result. Further attempts to communicate often leave them further apart rather than closer together.[1]

The differences may go unperceived by both parties, resulting perhaps in an illusion of understanding. We think we are transmitting truth, but our communication is being reprocessed by the hearer. Our words are interpreted according to his existing frame of reference. The result is that, instead of having an impact and producing change, our gospel is simply being synthesized into the listener's personal philosophy. In reality, he hasn't heard at all.

So we could say the primary communication task the team in Latin America faces is to close the gap successfully between themselves as communicators and the members of their audience. This requires two things: an understanding of the hearers' thought patterns, and the translation of the gospel message into their everyday language. The missionaries' message needs to be translated—out of North American Protestant terminology and communication forms—and into patterns which will be understood by Latin American students.

At this point you may be asking, "How does all this compare with what went on in the New Testament? How do we reconcile this with the phenomenal responses enjoyed by the early church in Acts?" This is what we will now consider.

Footnotes:
  1. Eugene A. Nida discusses this in *Message and Mission* (New York: Harper and Brothers, 1960), pages 89-90.

PART TWO:
Proclamation Evangelism

PROCLAIMING THE GOSPEL
Biblical, essential, and effective

AS STATED EARLIER, there are two primary modes of evangelism in the New Testament. The first is the *proclamation* of the gospel. This is an *action* through which the non-Christian receives a clear statement of the essential message. It is something that happens at a certain point in time—for example, during an evangelistic crusade. Another example would be a radio or television broadcast. A personal presentation of the gospel message to an individual belongs in this category. When someone declares the terms of man's reconciliation to God, the gospel has been proclaimed.

The Bible commands us to proclaim the gospel to the entire world, so whether we should engage in this is beyond discussion. Proclamation, however, must be used wisely if we expect to communicate the message to all kinds of peoples. Proclamation is mainly effective among a certain kind of people—the prepared.

Another mode of evangelism is necessary if we expect to reach significant numbers of the great majority of the world who do not possess a religious heritage. I call this second mode the *affirmation* of the gospel.

What is the affirmation of the gospel? It is a *process* of incarnating and demonstrating the Christian message. This approach is effective among the unprepared—that is, people without a Christian heritage and for whom Christianity does not constitute a credible basis for their lives. They are depending upon some "ism"—humanism, materialism, existentialism, socialism, or capitalism—to give coherence to their lives. With rare exceptions, drawing such individuals into the kingdom of God requires more than a summary statement of the gospel.

Both modes of evangelism—proclamation and affirmation—are essential if we are to evangelize those from a non-Christian environment as well as those who have a religious heritage. One cannot be judged better or more effective than the other. Both are essential and both are limited. The New Testament pattern seems to be that both should work together all the time. What is important for us to know is when to do what! To insist on using the mode of affirmation while a proclamation would suffice is a waste of effort. But to persist in proclaiming where more is required to get through is equally ineffective.

PROCLAIMING THE GOSPEL

Proclamation—the Greek word *kerusso* means to announce, to proclaim, to herald. This is the function of our daily newspaper or newscast. They announce the news. In the Roman context the word described the action of the announcer at the public games. But it would not be accurate to limit the meaning of proclamation to public preaching. It can take many forms, including individual, person-to-person persuasion.

In all four of the Gospels we are commanded to proclaim. In Matthew 24:14 Jesus said, "This gospel of the kingdom will be preached [*kerusso*] in the whole world." There are not just certain places in the world where it works to proclaim. We are to do it in *all* the world. Mark 13:10 is identical. The gospel must be preached [*kerusso*] to all nations. Mark 16:15 is even more specific: "Go into all the world and preach [*kerusso*] the good news to all creation." In Luke 24:47 the same word is used, and Luke tells us what the content of our proclamation should be. Jesus said we should proclaim "repentance and forgiveness of sins . . . to all nations."

Stop and think for a moment about what we expect to happen when we proclaim. Let's say we approach a twenty-four-year-old person with the intent of proclaiming the gospel to him. He has spent twenty-four years doing what he wanted to do, establishing habits, and developing his own value system. Almost everything he has fed into his mind is contrary to the word of God. Let's say we spend an hour with him during which we clearly explain the Christian faith. Now what do we expect to happen? We expect him to conclude that the direction he is taking in life is wrong. We expect him to say, "For twenty-four years I have been mistaken. In one hour you have shown me how to make an about-face in everything I have done until now."

Aren't we expecting the impossible? Yes, we are, but many times a day, all over the world, this conversation actually occurs. It is often effective. Why? There are several reasons.

In Acts 11:21 Luke reported that there were results when the gospel was proclaimed because *"the Lord's hand was with them."* This is important. This is what makes proclamation possible. If the Lord's hand is not with us, then we are, in fact, wasting our time. But the Bible says there are other reasons we can expect results from proclamation.

Acts 11:24 gives a second reason. It is because the pro- claimer (Barnabas) *"was a good man full of the Holy Spirit and faith."* That's a powerful trio: a good life, the Holy Spirit, and faith. There were results because of the quality of the message bearer.

In Acts 13:48, once again the gospel was being proclaimed

and as Luke wrote, the Holy Spirit explained why there were results: *"All who were appointed for eternal life, believed."* I understand this to mean that God has prepared certain people, who at the point of our encounter with them are ready to respond. We can expect to find at least some people like this almost everywhere we go.

But there are yet other reasons why we can expect results from proclamation. In Acts 14:1 Luke wrote, *"They spoke so effectively that a great number of Jews and Gentiles believed."* Then in Acts 16:14 we find still another reason. Referring to Lydia, Luke wrote *"The Lord opened her heart* to respond to Paul's message."

So we have a number of reasons to expect results from the proclamation of the gospel. We can expect the Lord's hand to be with us if we are men and women of faith and purity. We can expect to encounter some prepared people everywhere we go. We can learn how to share effectively. And we can expect the Lord to open people's hearts to respond.

SIX

THE HERITAGE FACTOR
Prerequisite for effective proclamation

THERE IS YET another reason why people respond to proclamation. Perhaps it is the predominant one.

There were two groups of people who responded to the proclamation of the gospel according to the account in Acts. The first was Jews. A Jew in the New Testament was a person who had sixteen centuries of religious heritage. God had given him the Scriptures—the law and the prophets. His system of government and his religion were one and the same.

The Jew was well-prepared. The celebration on the day of Pentecost brought *"God-fearing* Jews from every nation" to Jerusalem (Acts 2:5).

The second group was pagans who joined in the Jewish worship. They were known as "proselytes."

When God made his first move to spread the gospel to the Gentiles he singled out Cornelius, a Roman soldier whom Luke described as "devout and God-fearing" (Acts 10:2).

Then the missionary movement began. Paul was in Antioch serving the church there as one of five leaders. Barnabas was another. The Holy Spirit knew that Antioch could spare two of the five, so Paul and Barnabas were sent off as missionaries.

They followed a certain tactic everywhere they went. First they visited the synagogue. Obviously, almost everyone found in a synagogue would have some spiritual interest. Although these people had not heard about Christ, they were seeking after God according to their traditional patterns. They had the benefit of a religious heritage. The result was that many of them believed when Paul and Barnabas preached the gospel. Both Jews and proselyte Gentiles became Christians.

An unusual thing happened when they arrived in Philippi. There was no synagogue in that city. Apparently Paul and Barnabas heard there was a place by the river where people regularly met for prayer. They went there and discovered Lydia. But, again, she was a person who was "a worshiper of God" (Acts 16:14). Again they were taking the gospel to those who were prepared.

In Athens it was a different story (see Acts 17:16-34). Paul "was greatly distressed to see that the city was full of idols. So he reasoned in the synagogue with the Jews and the God-fearing Greeks, as well as in the marketplace day by day with those who happened to be there" (Acts 17:16-17). He even argued with the Epicurean and Stoic philosphers.

The philosophers were intrigued by his new teaching and took him to the Areopagus so he could give a discourse. This is the only recorded message given by Paul to a pagan crowd (people who did not have a religious heritage). Notice the difference in the content of his message. He did not appeal to the Old Testament: he was more philosophical. He even quoted the Greek poets. He started witnessing in a different way . . . he began with the person of God. Then he spoke about Jesus and the resurrection. The results were meager. "A few men became followers of Paul and believed" (Acts 17:34).

Compare the results of Paul's message with the results of

Peter's address on Pentecost found in Acts 2:37-41. What was the difference? Was Peter more Spirit-filled? Was Peter a better communicator? No. The difference was the Jews' religious heritage which prepared them to respond eagerly to the gospel.

Getting substantial results from proclamation presupposes some advance preparation of the hearers (planting and watering). Yet we are commanded to proclaim throughout the entire world. Why? Because we must assume God is at work preparing some in every place. *But he never intended us to limit our involvement in witnessing to efforts which only involve the method of proclamation.*

SEVEN

THE SCOPE OF PROCLAMATION

Limited effectiveness

PROCLAMATION IS COMMANDED. It is globally effective, but it is limited. It is limited as to the audiences it can reach as well as in its purpose.

The apostle Paul recognized this and consequently restricted himself to working within certain guidelines. This approach was essential to his success. He didn't try to do everything. He was primarily a proclaimer. He ranged his world proclaiming the gospel until he could make the amazing statement in his letter to the Romans, "So from Jerusalem all the way around to Illyricum, I have fully proclaimed the gospel of Christ. . . . But now that there is no more place for me to work in these regions, and since I have been longing for many years to see you, I plan to do so when I go to Spain" (Romans 15:19, 23-24).

What did Paul mean when he said he had finished his work? Did he mean he had evangelized every living person from Jerusalem to Illyricum? He couldn't have. His tactic was to go to a city, reap those who were prepared, establish them, and move on. What percentage of the population of a city like Corinth, the sin capital of the Roman Empire, had ever seen the inside of a Jewish synagogue? Only a fraction of the citizens had. But in many cities Paul's evangelistic outreach did not reach beyond the synagogue. On what basis could Paul claim he had finished his job in those places?

Paul wrote the Corinthians, "We, however, will not boast beyond proper limits, but will confine our boasting to the field God has assigned to us, a field that reaches even to you . . . neither do we go beyond our limits by boasting of work done by others. Our hope is that, as your faith continues to grow, our area of activity among you will greatly expand" (2 Corinthians 10:13-15). Paul was saying his sphere of ministry was to establish beachheads of new believers. He didn't do everything; he just established beachheads. Then he counted on the continued growth of his offspring to enlarge that sphere. The entire success of Paul's effort depended on the continued growth and subsequent expansion of the gospel through his spiritual children.

Often it was persecution that kept Paul moving, but even when he wasn't forced on, he didn't settle down for long. He would move on (Ephesus, where he stayed three years, was one exception) when the prepared were reaped and had received the basics of the faith.

In our contemporary evangelistic efforts we tend to want to emulate Paul, but we fail to complete the picture. We labor as if the gospel, once proclaimed to the world, has had a full opportunity to work. If we could just get the gospel to every person once in this generation, we think our job would be done. But we must recognize that even if we did achieve that goal, we would have only begun the job of evangelizing the world. Beachheads would be established, but the larger challenge would still be before us. We would have to admit that we were then only in a position from which to *begin* thoroughly evangelizing the world!

Our environments illustrate my meaning. Think for a minute. What percentage of your friends and acquaintances are reasonably close to the kingdom? How many would readily submit their lives to Christ if someone explained the gospel to them? What about the others? Are they beyond hope? If not, how could they be reached? Who will do it?

Not everyone is reachable, and not everyone is reapable. But once we recognize there is far more to evangelism than proclamation, we have at least acknowledged the need to use a variety of methods which should eventually allow everyone to at least hear the gospel message in a way they can understand. We live in a secularized world that we are scarcely influencing with the gospel. In part, the problem is a limited view of evangelism. We see it only as an activity: proclamation.

This view restricts the mobility of the gospel in two ways: It is limited, as to whom it will reach—only those with prior preparation, and as to who can do the proclaiming. Few middle-aged businessmen or housewives find themselves in an environment where proclamation can be a daily way of life. Sustained proclamation implies constant access to new groups of people. Jesus sent the twelve out two by two, but neither they nor their offspring spent their lives organizing similar expeditions.

Can our understanding of evangelism be complete if it does not realistically allow for the average Christian to enjoy a lifetime of personal involvement and fruitfulness?

EIGHT

THE PUZZLING EPISTLES
Where are the exhortations to witness?

Before reading this chapter, read the New Testament letters and note every exhortation about witnessing.

WE HAVE JUST observed how Paul limited his sphere of ministry to establishing beachheads of believers, usually in key centers. But his vision did not stop there. His work did, but his vision did not. He depended upon the ongoing growth of those little bodies of Christians for the preservation of his labors and the continued expansion of the gospel in the world. In fact, he maintained that if this did not occur, his labor would ultimately prove to have been for nothing (see Philippians 2:16).

This being the case—with so much resting on the performance of those little churches—one would expect Paul's letters to them to abound with exhortations to witness, to get out and continue what he had begun, proclaiming the gospel to every person. But no such exhortations are there! Why not? Perhaps it's because Paul realized that *merely more of the same would be counter-productive.* He had come in and reaped. Winning the remainder of those pagan societies required more than words. There had to be further planting and watering.

This is supported by what Paul did say in his letters about winning the lost. For example, he told Titus to "teach the older women to be reverent in the way they live . . . they can train the younger women to love their husbands and children, to be self-controlled and pure, to be busy at home, to be kind, and to be subject to their husbands, *so that no one will malign the word of God"* (Titus 2:3-5).

He urged him to "encourage the younger men to be self-controlled. . . . In your teaching show integrity, seriousness and soundness of speech . . . *so that those who oppose you may be ashamed because they have nothing bad to say about us"* (Titus 2:6-8).

Paul wanted Titus to "teach slaves to be subject to their masters in everything, to try to please them, . . . *so that in every way they will make the teaching about God our Savior attractive"* (Titus 2:9-10).

These cause and effect statements reveal Paul's clear understanding of the importance of the people of God *modeling* the character of God before sharing the gospel. Almost without fail, when he discussed the problem of the lost world, he focused on our "being" as the fundamental solution.

"Whatever happens, *conduct yourselves in a manner worthy of the gospel* of Christ. Then . . . I will know that you stand firm in one spirit, contending as one man for the faith of the gospel" (Philippians 1:27).

THE EXAMPLE OF SERGIO

Sergio was among the first generation of Christians who came from our university ministry in Brazil. He belonged to a family of industrialists who had established a reputation for not being concerned about honesty or integrity. Sergio was studying law and economics, preparing to assume the responsibility for the legal needs of his family's various business ventures.

Sergio had polio when he was four years old. He walked with a full body brace and crutches. He possessed an incredibly strong will, the result of his years of battling against the confines of his paralyzed body.

When we first met, he was a cold, hard person. We would meet once or twice weekly and drive to a favorite spot overlooking the city where we would study the Scriptures together. As he moved from his agnosticism to Jesus Christ, he began to change. By the time he was finishing his studies he was a mature Christian, and the changes in his personality were obvious to all who knew him.

But there was a problem. What was he going to do about his future? His family was putting him through school with the understanding that he was being prepared to work with them. But how could he do this without compromising his integrity? After all, wasn't it a lawyer's function to help the businessman get away with as much illegal activity as possible? I could see Sergio was disturbed about this, but I didn't know how to help him.

The year Sergio was to graduate from the university, Brazil went through a financial crisis that drove many businesses into bankruptcy. The industries belonging to Sergio's family were among these. Suddenly he was free from his obligations to work for his family. He was on his own.

The week he graduated he came to me and announced he had made two decisions. He had decided to put God first, and to be honest. With that he moved back to his hometown, rented an office, and opened his own law practice.

A few months later one of the local farmers was on the verge of losing his farm because of unpaid back taxes. The farm went up for public auction, and Sergio bought it. A murmur ran through the town, for the purchase appeared to be typical of the opportunism that characterized the rest of

Sergio's family. But what Sergio did next stopped the town in its tracks. He went to the farmer and gave him back the deed to his property, instructing him to repay the debt as he was able!

Sergio didn't have to do this. It was his legal right to keep the farm. But he acted with grace, not merely with justice— just as God does with us.

Sergio probably has another thirty-five years in business ahead of him. If he continues the way he has begun, the sheer influence of his life will go a long way toward breaking up the spiritual soil in that valley where he lives.

I learned a lot as I watched Sergio work out his discipleship in the context of his business. His foundational decisions to "put God first and to be honest" were strategic! Without that he would have neither a platform to witness from, nor a message backed by a Christian lifestyle. He could only look forward to living out his life with little hope of being used by God in others' lives.

Jesus said, "You will receive power when the Holy Spirit comes on you; and you will be my witnesses" (Acts 1:8). It seems to me this statement summarizes what we're saying in this chapter. The command is not to *do* witnessing, but to *be* Christ's witnesses. Evangelism is not merely an activity; it is a way of living. When we lose sight of this, if all we do is pro-claim, the people we win will not learn how to reproduce themselves spiritually. We must obey Christ's command to make disciples by "teaching them to obey everything I have commanded you" (Matthew 28:20). Or those we win will never go on and bear fruit themselves, and there will be no second crop. The harvest will be limited to that first cutting. But where *being* is in focus, the crop is perennial.

In the light of this, I hope you will take the time to review the New Testament epistles again and note all that they do say about our witness to the world.

NINE

AFFIRMATION IN ISRAEL
God's Chosen People

THERE IS ONE underlying purpose entwined in everything God is doing in relation to man. It can be summarized in one word: reconciliation. "God was reconciling the world to himself in Christ" (2 Corinthians 5:19). He committed the "message of reconciliation" to men. We've observed that God even divided the world into cultures and nations with reconciliation in mind.

The people of God have always been essential to the accomplishment of his purposes. Until we grasp this, we will never have an adequate understanding of evangelism—or of the Christian life.

ISRAEL: THE LEAST LIKELY

As a nation, Israel got off to an improbable start—it was the nation least likely to succeed. It all began with one man and a promise. Abraham was seventy-five years old and Sarah was sixty-six when they left Haran to seek the fulfillment of God's promise. After eleven years of desert life, when Abraham was eighty-six and Sarah seventy-seven, they lost their patience. The result was Ishmael. But he didn't count, and they were worse off than before.

They waited another fourteen years for Isaac, the son of the promise, to be born. By now Abraham was 100 years old and Sarah was 91. Forty years later Isaac married Rebekah. By then his mother had already died. Isaac and Rebekah waited twenty years for their twin sons, Jacob and Esau, to be born. But only one of the twins, Jacob, was to share the promise. So after eighty-five years, from God's calling of Abraham to Haran, to the birth of Jacob, the nation of Israel still consisted of only three people: Jacob and his parents.

Neither Jacob nor his mother were exactly models of integrity. Jacob deceived his father, swindled his brother, and fought with his uncle. His wives were idolators. But Jacob's family swelled into a clan of seventy people, a band of nomads with doubtful moral standards.

So after 225 years (during which they wandered from Haran to Egypt) the nation only consisted of one family of seventy people.

Next came 430 years of slavery in Egypt. They were years of silence on God's part: no miracles, no signs, no renewed promises. Not a sound from God. All Israel had to go on from the Lord over those centuries were the aging stories passed from father to son about a seemingly distant God who had occasionally visited their ancestors Abraham, Isaac, and Jacob. And now Israel was in slavery, hardly an environment conducive to cultural development.

Finally, under Moses' leadership, Israel fled Egypt as a nation numbering a million men. While wandering in the desert, Israel acquired a culture that was so sophisticated and comprehensive that it leaped centuries, leaving the neighboring nations behind in stark contrast. God gave Israel guidelines for medicine, hygiene, economics, agriculture, ethics, politics, law, and religion.

There were 655 years between the departure from Haran and the Exodus. That's a long time! If he was superimposed on our calendar, Abraham would be like a figure out of the Middle Ages. Why did God do it this way? The book of Deuteronomy gives us some clues. God was after more than Israel. He wanted the world.

Moses challenged the nation to think of this greater purpose when he told the people, "I have taught you decrees and laws . . . so that you may follow them in the land you are entering . . . Observe them carefully, for this will show your wisdom and understanding to the nations, who will hear about all these decrees and say, 'Surely this great nation is a wise and understanding people.' What other nation is so great as to have their gods near them the way the Lord our God is near us whenever we pray to him? And what other nation is so great as to have such righteous decrees and laws as this body of laws I am setting before you today?" (Deuteronomy 4:5-8).

God chose Israel, not because they were the best or the greatest, but because they were so unlikely. It was obvious that if anything ever came of them, it would have to be God's doing. "Understand, then, that it is not because of your righteousness that the Lord your God is giving you this good land to possess, for you are a stiff-necked people. . . . you provoked the Lord your God to anger. . . . From the day you left Egypt until you arrived here, you have been rebellious against the Lord" (Deuteronomy 9:6-7).

Israel was God's mouthpiece to the world. Judging from their history, the world would have to recognize that the living God had, in fact, taken up with this nation. That was precisely the point. It worked. By the time of King Solomon, he "was greater in riches and wisdom than all the other kings of the earth. The whole world sought audience with Solomon to hear the wisdom God had put in his heart" (1 Kings 10:23-24).

God made an alliance with Israel. He so identified himself with her that he was known in the world as "the God of Israel." And how Israel prospered through this relationship!

She became beautiful, because she reflected the personality of God himself. The world beat a path to her door.

All went well as long as the people of Israel were obedient to God's commandments. But God made himself vulnerable through this alliance. Israel possessed the power to mislead the entire world! All she had to do was disobey God or embrace her neighbor's gods and she would garble God's image before the world. The world would begin to draw wrong conclusions about him. And that's what happened.

This explains why God was so intolerant of her idolatry and why he withdrew his name and his presence from her as dramatically as he gave them. Moses taught the Israelites that if they rebelled and experienced God's judgment, then "all the nations will ask· 'Why has the Lord done this to this land? Why this fierce, burning anger?' And the answer will be: 'It is because this people abandoned the covenant of the Lord'" (Deuteronomy 29:24-25).

God had to make it clear to the world that he was not a party to Israel's injustices or perversions. Through Ezekiel the prophet God said, "They will know that I am the Lord when I disperse them among the nations and scatter them through the countries. But I will spare a few of them from the sword, famine and plague, so that in the nations where they go they may acknowledge all their detestable practices. Then they will know that I am the Lord" (Ezekiel 12:15-16).

In her obedience, Israel glorified God. That is, she served to reflect the nature of God to the world. God's attributes were incarnated by his people. She was a flesh and blood phenomenon for all to see. Because Israel existed, the world could no longer plead ignorance of God and his ways.

TEN

AFFIRMATION IN THE CHURCH
A unique people

"YOU THOUGH A wild olive shoot, have been grafted in among the others and now share in the nourishing sap from the olive root" (Romans 11:17). This is the church, the new people of God, but rooted in the same promises and fulfilling the same purposes as ancient Israel once did.

Israel collapsed and no longer functioned as a positive voice in the world. As she decayed, most of her people moved in one of two directions. Some, using the beauty and wealth with which God endowed the nation, fed their appetites to the extent that perversion, injustice, and corruption became the predominant national characteristics (see Ezekiel 16).

Others, the devout, were horrified by this abandonment of the old values, and purposed to be the heroic remnant—the preservers of the faith. They expanded on Moses' five books with a seventy-volume commentary, and kept the administrative structure of seventy elders which he had set up intact (see Exodus 18). Bent on maintaining the old standards, they fell into the trap of dead works (see Malachi 1-2). And the sect of the Pharisees was born.

It is amazing how anything as beautiful as Israel once was could become so ugly. It was a toss-up as to which extreme was most disgusting, the irreverent or the legalists. Both had an adverse impact on the world (see Romans 2:24).

But God's plan did not change. Through his own Son, he generated a new people, grafting them into the same rich root from which Israel had grown.

The beginnings were parallel: twelve sons of Jacob, twelve apostles. But the pace was different. What took 225 years with Israel, Christ accomplished in a little over three years. Jacob left a clan of seventy in Egypt, while Jesus left a body of 120 in a room in Jerusalem. Just as God distinguished Israel with a unique culture, so did Jesus with the church. But here we observe a marked contrast. While Israel's culture was sociopolitical in nature, the sphere of this new people was fundamentally spiritual.

THE CHURCH: THE OUTPOST OF THE KINGDOM OF GOD

Jesus came preaching the kingdom of God. It was the first thing he talked about and the last. Even though he made the kingdom his primary theme, few, if any, clearly grasped its significance. We can hardly blame them, as his words still seem obscure and often enigmatic.

He described the kingdom as being present, yet future; revealed, yet a mystery; among us, yet not of this world; like a small seed, yet pervading everything. He compared it to a net full of fish, twenty virgins, a treasure hidden in a field, and a pearl merchant.

The apostles betrayed their lack of insight about the kingdom in their very last conversation with Jesus, just before he ascended. They asked if he wasn't about to fulfill their expectations by restoring Israel's political order. They failed to grasp the true scope of the kingdom. They failed to realize that

Jesus, in his teachings, was introducing a truly radical order. He was introducing a new life-style with new values, new attitudes, new relationships—in short, a new culture: the kingdom culture!

It is in understanding what Jesus teaches us about citizenship in God's kingdom that the radical uniqueness of the Christian life dawns on us. His words are to us what the book of Leviticus was to Israel. Jesus intends for his people, the church, to model "life in the kingdom."

E. Stanley Jones observed that the kingdom of God is really a totalitarian order, and not like human systems which must content themselves with outward conformity. The kingdom of God reaches to our inmost thoughts. One cannot think a thought without the approval or disapproval of the kingdom. The kingdom also ranges to the outermost rim of our relationships.[1] This sounds like bondage! But the effect is the reverse of man's authoritarian systems. Rather than enslaving people, entering the kingdom culture and practicing a kingdom lifestyle liberates them.

Perhaps Jesus' words seem so obscure because they oppose the world's value system. We read his teachings, and we understand the sentences, but we conclude that somehow he couldn't really have meant what he said.

For now, the important thing to recognize is that just as God raised up Israel to amplify his voice through the world, he has assigned us the same function. Peter's words repeated what the Israelites had been taught centuries earlier: "You are a chosen people, a royal priesthood, a holy nation, a people belonging to God, that you may declare the praises of him who called you out of darkness into his wonderful light. . . . Live such good lives among the pagans that . . . they may see your good deed and glorify God on the day he visits us" (1 Peter 2:9,12).

SUMMARY

Paul's emphasis on our *being* is supported by the sweep of Scripture. The existence of a unique people, whose lives are marked by God himself, has always been fundamental to his program of reconciling the world to himself. His people incarnate his character; they audio-visualize the nature of his eternal reign.

How this works out in practice has been, and is, one of the most difficult issues the church struggles with. The pendulum has steadily swung back and forth for 2,000 years between the extremes of isolation and compromise.

Footnotes:

1. E. Stanley Jones, *A Song of Ascents* (Nashville, Tennessee: Abingdon Press, 1968; Festival edition, 1979), pages 151-152.

====================ELEVEN====================

A GOOD TESTIMONY
Often just a legalistic caricature

WHEN HE WAS thirteen years old, my son Todd asked, "Dad, how can I be a good testimony? I'm not as good a Christian as Michelle (his older sister). She's talking to her friends about Christ."

My mind flashed back to the time I was thirteen. I remembered how I had been caught between two unreconciliable desires. I had wanted to measure up to what I imagined my parents expected of me so far as having a Christian testimony among my friends, but at the same time I had to meet my needs for approval among my peers. I remembered the guilt and tension this conflict caused me. Now, how could I help my son avoid the same problem?

Finally I said, "Todd, don't worry about words. Just concern yourself with one thing. Be a peacemaker." I explained that if he would be genuinely considerate of the other person and if he would take the initiative in resolving the conflicts that arose, he would be doing what God wants of him. This was something my thirteen-year-old could handle.

A few weeks later Todd had an argument with Eduardo, our neighbor's boy, and their friendship broke up. When Todd and I talked about this incident, we reviewed our discussion on being a peacemaker and read Romans 12:17-18 together: "Do not repay anyone evil for evil. Be careful to do what is right in the eyes of everybody. If it is possible, as far as it depends on you, live at peace with everyone." Todd decided to take the initiative, visited Eduardo, and restored their friendship.

Soon after that, Eduardo's mother invited my wife over to her home to talk. She explained that her family had observed Todd's friendship with Eduardo and concluded, "We think you have what we need." A thirteen-year-old's life opened the door to another family.

The witness of a life! It is a truth rooted in God's purposes for Israel and in the teachings of the apostles. "Our gospel came to you not simply with words, but also with power, with the Holy Spirit and with deep conviction. You know how we lived among you for your sake" (1 Thessalonians 1:5).

This great truth has been reduced to the phrase "having a good testimony." But the phrase doesn't fit. In fact, this truth is sometimes further restricted in practice to mean merely reinforcing the caricature that both Christians and non-Christians share of what a "good Christian" should look like. This caricature consists of those extrabiblical scruples that always seem to grow up around Christian groups. We are afraid that if we do not live up to the expected image, we will offend those in the group as well as non-Christians. This fear maintains the caricature. The observant non-Christian picks up the cue—and holds the Christian accountable for living up to his own criteria.

This is enough to virtually canonize that caricature of what it means to be a Christian. As a result, the sad truth is we effectively bar access to the gospel for many otherwise interested people.

WHAT IS NOT A GOOD TESTIMONY

"What must I forsake?" a young man asked.

"Colored clothes for one thing. Get rid of everything in your wardrobe that is not white. Stop sleeping on a soft pillow. Sell your musical instruments and don't eat any more white bread. You cannot, if you are sincere about obeying Christ, take warm baths or shave your beard. To shave is to lie against him who created us, to attempt to improve on his work."[1]

Quaint, isn't it—this example of extrabiblical scruples. And perhaps amusing. The list has contantly shifted over the 1,800 years since this one was written. It has even changed in my generation. It also varies with who and where you are in the world. But in spite of the relative nature of our standards for Christian conduct, we always tend to take them very seriously.

It seems that moralisms (human standards imposed as norms) inevitably emerge to threaten the dynamic in every expression of the body of Christ. There are a number of reasons for this, but we will not concern ourselves with them here. Our concern is the effect moralisms have on the gospel's mobility in the world. Jesus maintained that the Pharisees "shut the kingdom of heaven in men's faces" with their teachings (Matthew 23:13). Whenever the emphasis is on what Christians *do*, rather than what they *are*, this will be the effect to a greater or lesser degree.

Jesus spoke about this in the Sermon on the Mount. He said, "Let your light shine before men, that they may see your good deeds and praise your Father in heaven" (Matthew 5:16). Later in the same discourse, he seemed to contradict himself when he said, "Be careful not to do your 'acts of righteousness' before men, to be seen by them" (Matthew 6:1).

What was the difference between these two statements? Their contexts set them apart.

Jesus' first statement introduced the thought that we should live in such a way that people see God in us. Here his emphasis is on our *uniqueness in relating to people and situations.*

The context of the second statement has to do with activities: giving, praying, and fasting. Jesus did not say, Don't do these things. He commanded us to do all three. What he said was, Don't let anyone catch you at it! Why not? The answer relates to the motives of the heart. If my Christian activities are the most visible element of my faith, I'm probably guilty of glorifying myself. Consequently, I'm bound to misrepresent God. Outsiders will never want to come in once this begins to happen. Who wants to quit eating, give his money away, and spend all his time on his knees just to go to a heaven he's not even sure he will like?

We do the gospel considerable injustice when we attempt to promote our faith by publicizing our scruples, promoting our church activities, or describing our devotional lives. If, after all this, someone still found the idea appealing, they would probably think, *Perhaps I should be a Christian too, but how would I find the time?*

BEING FULL OF GRACE AND TRUTH

What then is a good testimony? An individual with a good testimony is one who models the character of God. "We have seen his glory . . . full of grace and truth" (John 1:14). What a beautiful, irresistible figure! Not that of a legalistic caricature, but the reflection of the very person of God. I believe that is what it means to glorify God. It is to reveal his person.

Grace and truth, mercy and justice—these are the inseparable marks of God's person. In Ephesians 4:15 we are told to "speak the *truth* in *love*," a similar couplet. Truth without love destroys. Love without truth deceives.

BEHAVING AS SONS OF THE TRUTH

Even Jesus' enemies acknowledged his commitment to truth. On one occasion, in a preface to a trap question, they made the observation, "Teacher . . . we know you are a man of integrity and that you teach the way of God in accordance with the truth. You aren't swayed by men, because you pay no attention to who they are" (Matthew 22:16). As members of his body, we are called upon to imitate Christ by being honest. As Peter wrote about Jesus, "No deceit was found in his mouth" (1 Peter 2:22).

What does truth have to do with being a good testimony? For one thing, almost all of our world's social problems, from broken marriages to poverty, have their roots in selfishness and greed. The problems begin in the heart of man, so the solutions must also begin there. The opposite of selfishness is doing what is right even when it is to your disadvantage (see Psalm 15). That is integrity. One of the most fundamental needs in this world is for men and women of integrity. And if integrity isn't found among the people of God, where will it be found? When the Christian models integrity, he affirms to the world that there is a better way of doing things.

GRACE

We can only exercise the grace of God in our relationships with others. Have you ever noticed how much emphasis Jesus gave to the quality of our relationships? When asked to identify the greatest of God's commands, he replied that all of the law can be summed up with two statements, each involving a relationship: "Love the Lord your God with all your heart and with all your soul and with all your mind. . . . and love your neighbor as yourself" (Matthew 22:37-39).

Much of what Jesus had to say in his Sermon on the Mount consists of a call for us to be redemptive in our relationships. Consider this paraphrase.

"You have heard it said, 'Do not murder.' I say don't be angry with your brother.

"You have heard it said, 'Don't be contemptuous of others.' I say don't even belittle another.

"Be reconciled to your brother even before you stop to commune with God.

"Settle matters quickly with your adversary, and out of court.

"Anyone who looks at a woman lustfully has already committed adultery with her in his heart.

"You have heard it said, 'eye for eye and tooth for tooth.' But I tell you, do not resist an evil person.

"Give to the one who asks you, and do not turn away from the one who wants to borrow from you.

"You have heard that it was said, 'Love your neighbor and hate your enemy' But I tell you: Love your enemies and pray for those who persecute you, that you may be sons of your Father . . . perfect, therefore, as your heavenly Father is perfect" (see Matthew 5:1-7:29).

These are difficult statements to cope with. They seem impossible to put into practice. But that's the way the grace of God always appears—impossible, just the opposite of what we instinctively "know" to be right, whether it is on the level of faith versus works for salvation, or unfairness versus justice in the day-by-day affairs of life.

Grace, by nature, is what a person least deserves. That's how God relates to us, and that's how he wants us, in turn, to respond to others. Insight into this truth of the grace of God—as we receive it and as we exercise it—could be called the starting point of all spiritual progress. As Paul wrote, "This gospel is producing fruit and growing . . . among you since the day you heard it and understood God's grace in all its truth" (Colossians 1:6).

All our natural inclinations run contrary to this great truth. Paul Tournier, the Swiss psychiatrist and author, observed that our tendency is to be lenient or indulgent toward our own weaknesses (I'm overweight because it runs in my family) while bringing others to account (why doesn't he discipline his eating?).[2] There needs to be a reversal here.

Perhaps in part, the word *conversion* implies turning this around. To do this means to seek to understand *why* another individual is the way he is, and to make allowances accordingly, while holding ourselves responsible for our own behavior. This is the message of the "forgiveness chapter," Matthew 18. "Shouldn't you have had mercy on your fellow servant just as I had on you?" (Matthew 18:33). The chapter ends on a sobering note: "In anger his master turned him over to the jailers until he should pay back all he owed. This is how my heavenly Father will treat each of you unless you forgive your brother from your heart" (Matthew 18:34-35).

Unforgiving words on forgiveness! How can that be? I wonder if Jesus isn't saying, If you do not forgive or exercise grace in your dealings with people, it is a sure sign you never understood the cross!

To be treated with grace is to taste redemption. Have you ever found yourself being accepted and understood when you expected and deserved just the opposite? It's overwhelming. But to act graciously toward someone else is even better.

So we may conclude that a "good testimony" is a person whose quality of life identifies him as a child of his heavenly Father, full of grace and truth. Like his Father, he is redemptive in his relationships, from the inner circle within his own family to the outer fringes where his enemies stand.

Footnotes:
1. Elisabeth Elliot, *The Liberty of Obedience* (Waco, Texas: Word Books, 1968), pages 45-46.
2. Paul Tournier, *The Person Reborn* (New York: Harper and Row, 1966), pages 128-129.

TWELVE

MODELING AN EFFECTIVE OPTION

Demonstrating the Christian life

WE HAVE SEEN that a person with a good testimony is one who is redemptive in his relationships. Wherever he goes he sows life and hope rather than despair, conflict, or death. As such, the Christian is the most significant figure in our society. Jesus called him the salt of the earth, the light of the world, and the good seed. He is a singular exception in a disoriented world.

About the time the Watergate scandal was being revealed, I was on a plane going into Washington, D.C. I was engrossed in a book on politics, quite oblivious to the person seated next to me. Evidently what I was reading stirred his interest because he initiated a conversation with me about the book. I soon learned he was an attorney assigned to negotiating labor disputes. Our conversation drifted to Watergate, and I asked him what he thought its root causes were. He replied that it reflected "incompetence in leadership, and isolation from reality at the top.''

I said I felt at least one other factor had to be included, and that was the absence of moral absolutes. He didn't understand what I was saying, so I illustrated it with the story of a California lawsuit.

In the early sixties, several restaurant owners in California began employing topless waitresses. The local citizens filed suit against the owners, charging them with immoral conduct. When the citizens won their case in the state courts, the restaurant owners appealed the decision to the U.S. Supreme Court. There they got a reversal on the state court's decision and were given the legal right to continue operating with topless waitresses.

I pointed out to my companion that the disturbing thing about this case was the basis upon which it was won by the restaurant operators. The decision (along with a few other contemporary cases) set a precedent in American law that continues to undermine the entire system. The restaurant owners won their case with this argument: Our topless restaurants are frequented by some of the leading citizens in the community; therefore, what takes place reflects the community's moral standards. Since the citizens of a community are the ones who should determine its moral standards, what is going on in those retaurants is *right*.

I explained that once we concede the assumption that it is the citizens who determine what is right and wrong, we have cut ourselves adrift in a sea of relativism. To dramatize the fallacy: Using the same argument, those leading citizens could decide they don't like Spanish-speaking people or any other group and justify killing them.

Returning to the Watergate case, I reminded my companion of the repeated explanation by the defendants that they were just doing what they felt would accomplish their goal—keeping President Richard Nixon in office. I explained that once "right" becomes whatever contributes to the prevailing goals, the ultimate result is disintegration. He saw my point and agreed. So the two of us sat there for a few moments contemplating the unfortunate fact that since absolutes no longer exist in our society, our survival is compromised.

Finally, inevitably, he asked, "What absolutes would you suggest?"

I said, "I'm a Christian."

He couldn't see what this had to do with it, so I went on to explain. "Let us suppose for a moment that both you and I were Christians. That would mean we both believe in a God. If we could accept that, he would be an absolute, wouldn't he?"

My companion agreed.

I continued, "But even if God existed, it wouldn't do us any good unless we had some word from him as to what life is all about, would it?"

Again he agreed.

I went on. "That's exactly what the Bible is—a word from God as to what life is about. So as Christians, you and I would have two absolutes: God and his word. That would be an adequate basis of truth for us to operate on, don't you think?" This launched us into a dynamic discussion about Jesus Christ.

It is true that collectively man cannot thrive without moral absolutes. It is just as true, but perhaps less apparent on the individual level.

A few years ago our family moved into a new neighborhood during a temporary stay in the United States. One of our first friendships was with a young couple who lived down the block and across the street from us. While we were out for dinner together one evening, my wife and I told them we were thinking of inviting some of our neighbors to discuss common problems in marriage, the family, and other human relationships, using the Bible as our basis. They reacted enthusiastically. The husband said, "I think I could get everyone on the block to come. We don't know of a single couple in this neighborhood who could be called happy."

Ours is, in fact, a neurotic society. Problems and tensions in society are widespread, while on the individual level man is asking survival questions: How do I cope with feelings of futility and insecurity? How do I get along with this woman? What should we do with our children?

Answers to questions such as these will not be forth-coming from either our social scientists or our philosophers. France's "new philosophers," mirroring our times, say all ideologies are dangerous delusions. They, and others, have concluded that there really are no answers to man's basic questions. With this conclusion they are probably closer to the truth now than secular man has ever been!

In Isaiah 50:11 God says, "All you who light fires and pro-vide yourselves with flaming torches, go, walk in the light of your fires and of the torches you have set ablaze. This is what you shall receive from my hand: You will lie down in tor-ment."

When Jesus said, "I am the truth," it was good news in-deed. He is our reference point, allowing the Christian to walk through the ruins of man-made philosophies on a true course. As he walks in the light, in the truth that is Christ himself, the Christian is a statement from God to the world that there *is* another option.

THIRTEEN

CONGRUENCE OF LIFE AND BELIEF
The Christian value system

"YOU WERE ONCE darkness, but now you are light in the Lord. Live as children of light" (Ephesians 5:8). Being light presupposes congruence: harmony between God's ways and our own. One thing that disrupts this harmony is the constant, subtle, often subliminal influences our society exerts on us.

Jesus was speaking to this danger in his comments on leaven (yeast). He warned his disciples to "beware of the leaven of the Pharisees and Sadducees" (Matthew 16:6 RSV) "and the leaven of Herod" (Mark 8:15 RSV). Leaven symbolizes human imperfection (see Exodus 12:15-20, 13:3-8, Leviticus 2:11, 1 Corinthians 5:6-8). Jesus was warning against mixing imperfect human ideas with God's truth. The Pharisees had mixed their own religious traditions with the Scriptures; the Sadducees were the philosophers of Jewish society; and Herod represented the world system. These three influences—tradition, philosophy, and society—seem inevitably to work their way into and become part of the value system of any Christian community to such an extent that it is possible to be a Christian, but live almost entirely within a pagan value system, and *not even perceive it.*

This possibility began to dawn on me when we moved to Brazil and changed cultures. Culture is hardly perceived as long as we do not leave the only one we really know. A fish doesn't perceive the water it swims in, and neither are we aware of our culture, or the influence it exerts on our thoughts and actions. Often we must step outside of it to understand it—and to understand ourselves!

I have since learned that this experience is common to those who cross cultural lines. One acquaintance, Bob Malcolm, who spent many years as a missionary in the Philippines observed, "I spent most of my time in the Philippines trying to sort out which of my beliefs were American, which beliefs were Filipino, and which were Christian. I came to the conclusion that much of what I believed belonged to the first two categories."

As we moved into the Brazilian culture, we gradually became aware of the origins of our value system. I was chagrined to discover that much of my "biblical Christianity" did not really come from the Bible at all. My attitude toward work and material things came out of cultural distortions of the Puritan work ethic. My thinking processes and my approach to problem solving were marked by the computer revolution. Marketing and consumerism had influenced my definition and evaluation of progress. Madison Avenue and television had helped to set my living standard. I found I had a greater disposition for violence than the people we were ministering to, a result of our American history. My philosophy of child-raising was affected by humanism. Even women's liberation and the Beatles had affected me. What a shock to realize the collage my supposedly biblical Christianity really was. I was a sub-Christian Christian!

As this dawned on me, I asked myself, Is this the message I'm going to pass on to my Brazilian friends? I thought I needed to "Brazilianize" my Christianity. But I soon realized that also would be sub-Christian because all human systems are marred.

It was at this point in my thinking that the phrase "kingdom of God" began to get my attention. For me the kingdom had always been one of those things to skip over in the Bible. It seemed distant, among the more impractical Bible truths. But now, for some reason I began to mark the word *kingdom* with ink every time I ran across it in my Bible. I was still at it two years later, but didn't know why. Whenever I would attempt to tell others what I was learning on the subject, I'd go blank—a sure sign I hadn't put the pieces together. I asked God for help to clear it up for me, because by then the kingdom seemed to be standing out on every page. *Surely such a predominant theme was significant!*

Then I realized this was the third option! Not an Americanized Christianity, nor a Brazilianized Christianity, but a Christianity growing out of the culture of the kingdom—the kingdom culture! Not a provincial, flawed, human order, but God's untarnished, universal domain, a whole new way of living. There it was, beautifully laid out by God for his people. When the unique kingdom culture comes into focus, the incongruities in one's life, the areas that had previously escaped the redemptive process, are called into account. No other biblical truths call our attention to the radical uniqueness of the Christian life as do the teachings on the kingdom.

It was in the context of Jesus' words about the kingdom that he spoke about the dangers of leaven. Where does leaven come from? Jesus described the leavening sequence in Mark 7:6-13. He pointed out that the process begins with a good idea. It is so good, in fact, we agree it should become a norm, a rule. Consequently, a man's idea gains equal weight with the word of God.

The next stop is neglecting the word of God while still adhering to that good idea. By now the idea has become a tradition. We soon find the tradition more to our liking than the word of God, so we set his word aside. Finally, the tradition comes full circle. Jesus said, "You nullify the word of God by your tradition" (verse 13). This happens when our practice actually works against doing the will of God.

To illustrate, let's take one of the most successful and beneficial forms that exist in our churches—the Sunday school. The Sunday school is a good idea.

Originally the Sunday school was brought into being as a means of teaching children who did not have Christian parents, children who would have had little opportunity to receive the gospel. In those early days no self-respecting Christian parent would send his child to Sunday school, as it would be an admission of failure on his part. He would be considered negligent of his responsibility to teach his own children as we are told to do in Deuteronomy 6:6-7: "These commandments . . . are to be upon your hearts. Impress them on your children. Talk about them when you sit at home and when you walk along the road, when you lie down and when you get up."

Apparently the benefits of the Sunday school were so evident that the attitude of the Christian parents changed. Soon no self-respecting Christian would neglect sending his children to Sunday school.

The next step is predictable. Dad neglects his scriptural responsibility for instructing his children in God's word and turns it over to the church—a responsibility the church simply cannot fulfill. The church cannot fulfill it because it is a parental responsibility. The Sunday school can contribute, but it can't assume what only Dad can do.

This sequence follows Jesus' description in Mark 7. When Dad lets go of his responsibility, disaster very often strikes him! His felt need for maintaining a godly life, for developing his mastery of the Scriptures, and his ability to teach them drops off. When he delegates responsibility for his family, he's free to wander.

If there's any one thing that prods me into maintaining mental and spiritual discipline, it's the realization that my children and their children will inherit the fruit of my thought life.

Holiness seems very sensible when seen from this angle (see Deuteronomy 4:39-40).

So how does it happen that incongruities leaven our Christianity? To summarize: "The Good News is converted into behavior and behavior into habit. The habit can become mere custom and quite irrelevant. Similarly *faith* tends to become *creed* and creed ends up as mere recitation."[1]

Now what does this matter of congruence—that is, harmony with God's ways—have to do with reaching the unreachable? It has a great deal to do with it. A congruent life is the secret of naturalness in communication. And naturalness is the secret of attracting rather than repelling with our witness. On the other hand, where there are incongruities in our lives we usually have to resort to devices or gimmicks to get our message across.

We must ask ourselves, Where did I get my opinions on everything: finances, success, marriage, child raising, business, time use, sex, people, pleasure, education, progress, society, sports, politics, organization, and religion? Did any of my beliefs come, in fact, from God's word? It is not acceptable for the Christian to borrow from the world's value system. As J.B. Phillips translated Romans 12:2, "Don't let the world around you squeeze you into its own mold, but let God remake you so that your whole attitude of mind is changed."

If we can trace our value system in these areas back to the word of God, communicating our faith becomes infinitely easier. Any subject, if explored far enough, will lead us into a discussion of the good news. We must always be prepared to explain why we are the way we are (see 1 Peter 3:15).

In my early Christian life, when I first began witnessing to my friends, the great hurdle was always getting started. I never seemed to know what to say. I began keeping a page of "openers" in a notebook. These were questions I would ask to get me into the subject. They included: "Was there ever a time in your life when you seriously considered becoming a Christian?" "What did you think of the sermon?" "Are you interested in spiritual things?"

Such questions can help. But they often backfired on me. I could never seem to get the timing right. I would "casually" throw these questions out in the midst of an otherwise normal conversation. At that point everything became abnormal. My quarry would tense up—and become almost as tense as I was. Then, electrically, I would go into my presentation. This approach was just as alien as the opening question. It consisted of heavy offers of eternal life and vague references to happiness now. Where there is incongruence, that's about all we have to offer. What we represent is not substantially any different from what the receiver already has. Even eternal life is not particularly attractive to him. He's already ambivalent about the life he does have—both hating and loving it, but not loving it enough to want it to go on forever.

A few years ago I had been away from home for many weeks on a long trip and had been with people constantly. I was desperate to get away from people for a while. So when I got on the plane I sat in an aisle seat. The middle seat was vacant and the window seat was occupied by a young woman. As I waited for the plane to take off, I retreated as deeply as possible into a book I was carrying. It was purely an anti-social maneuver. But my traveling companion wanted to talk. She asked, "What are you reading?"

"A book," I replied.

"What is the name of it?" she asked.

"*Psycho-Cybernetics* by Maxwell Maltz," I said.

"Do you study psychology?"

"No."

Everything was monosyllables. By then the engines were running and we were beginning to taxi down the runway. She kept at it. I had a head cold and could hardly hear. Finally, I closed the book and moved to the vacant seat between us, and we began to converse.

I soon realized what she really had in mind was to find a companion. Going straight to the point, I said, "I travel a lot and many times I am lonely. I often encounter temptations to be unfaithful to my wife. But I've decided it's not worth it. I know I could deceive her, but the basis of our relationship is our mutual love and confidence. She trusts me, and I trust her.

"I've lived long enough to realize that meaning in life is not found in seeing what I can get away with, or in bigger achievements, or in a position, or in how my leisure time is spent. I've learned that meaning is found in relationships. Consequently, I don't intend to destroy the best relationship I have. If I came home having been unfaithful to my wife, even though she might not perceive it, and even though I could keep it from her, I'd know. She would come to me with her blind confidence and I'd have to somehow create a distance between us. We'd be pulled apart and she would never know why. Soon we would be strangers living together under the same roof."

"The ones who would pay most heavily would be my wife and children. That strikes me as the height of self-ishness."

She was dumbfounded!

Then she began to open up. She said, "I'm twenty-four years old. I ought to be getting married, but all my married friends have affairs and if that's the way it is, I don't want it. When my friends go away for a weekend, their husbands are soon knocking at my door. They are like little boys. I just don't think I could handle it if my husband were like that."

Then she added, "I've never heard ideas like yours. Where do they come from?"

"You'd laugh if I told you."

"No, I wouldn't," she said.

"I got them from the Bible," I said. I went on to explain to her what the Christian message is and how it changes a person so he can get his life in order. By then we were about to land. What frustration! We were in the middle of my explanation. She was intensely interested in every word, but we had to quit.

As the passengers moved into the aisle, I let her go on ahead. When I came off a bit later and walked up the concourse, I passed her standing with a circle of about ten of her friends who had come to meet her. They were the ones she had told me about on the plane. She stopped me and made the round of introductions. I stood there for at least ten minutes while she related our conversation to them. That just added to my frustration. I thought, If only I had a few days with these people. Perhaps I could help change their darkness into light. I felt indispensable, but I had to go on my way.

But God was preparing me for one more big lesson. God is the one who orchestrates the reconciliation of people to himself, not us. Just one year later I was back in that same city. It was a Sunday morning, and I was seated in a church. In walked the same woman I had talked to on the airplane. She sat down directly in front of me. When the service was over, I stood up to introduce myself. It was unnecessary. Her reply was, "Of course, I remember. I'll never forget that conversation. What a difference it has made!"

This story illustrates how having values rooted in the Scriptures will enable us to turn almost any conversation into a discussion of the gospel.

But, I must confess, I still have apprehensions when I see a new neighbor move in, when we move to another city, or I meet a stranger. My first reaction is often anxious; How will I ever get to that person? He doesn't look like the type. At these times I have to remind myself there is no barrier that making his acquaintance won't resolve. Eventually, a conversation over dinner or some leisure time together will lead us to a spiritual discussion there. We'll have to talk about *something*. And all conversations eventually lead to Jesus Christ.

Melker, a first century priest, described the ideal. "The kingdom of God is to begin with us, in the inner life, and rule there, and from the inner nature all outward actions are to flow in conformity with revealed and written teachings and commands of God. . . . Until the outward is like the inward; and thus advancing on from individuals to nations."[2]

Footnotes:
1. The source for this quote has been misplaced in the author's files.

2. Letter of Melker, first century Priest of the Synagogue of Bethlehem to the Higher Sanhedrim of the Jews at Jerusalem, translated by Dr. McIntosh and Dr. Twyman, *The Archko Volume* (New Canaan, Connecticut: Keats Publishing Inc., 1975), pages 71-72.

FOURTEEN

PULL TOWARD ISOLATION
When separation becomes isolation

"IF YOU'RE PART of the evangelical sub-culture, it's your whole life. . . .You go to church, you buy the religious books, you watch the television programs. But if you're not part of the sub-culture, you never know it exists," according to Martin Marty, a divinity professor at the University of Chicago, as quoted in an article entitled "Old Time Religion" on the front page of *The Wall Street Journal* on July 11, 1980.

This article emphasized the degree to which evangelical Christians are isolated from the world around them. The subtitles reveal the reporter's conclusions:

An Evangelical Revival is Sweeping the Nation but
with Little Effect
Shunning the Sinful World
Effect Has Been Small
Shying From Involvement
The Journal's staff reporter, Jonathan Kauffman,

writes: "The current evangelical revival has so far sowed little except curiosity among nonbelievers. . . . the movement has affected American society far less than the Great Awakening of the mid-1700s." He also notes the "historical tendency for evangelicals to shy away from involvement in the secular, sinful world."

The distance between the church and the world was brought to my attention by some early experiences in Brazil. Soon after Osvaldo, (the Brazilian student who was unmoved by my two-hour gospel presentation) became a Christian, we invited him to move into our home. He lived with us for three years. While we taught him all we could about following God and obeying the Scriptures, he taught us all he could about Brazil's language and culture. The benefits were mutual.

As Osvaldo grew in his love for God, the relationship between the two of us also grew. He soon became a faithful friend. As I observed this progress, I decided it was time to begin taking him to church with us. It was Osvaldo's first exposure to Protestantism. Everything seemed to go fine. He never discussed his reactions, but he always went with us. I began to observe, however, that he was struggling.

One Sunday as we were walking home, I said, "Osvaldo, you don't really enjoy going to church, do you?" That opened the door! Out came the quesions: "Why do they express themselves so strangely?" "Why do they sing like that?" "Why do they change their voices when they pray?" And on and on. His questions were sincere; he was just looking for answers. But they irritated me. My attempts to answer him also irritated me, because I didn't do very well.

The incident passed, but Osvaldo's questions stuck. Because of them, I began to see those services through the eyes of an outsider. I had to concede that almost insurmountable communication problems existed on both sides. The outsider would never feel at home until he submitted himself to a series of modifications in his customs and lifestyle. And the congregation was not willing to extend their fellowship to him until it was evident these changes were taking place.

Sometimes it is possible for a new Christian to accept this process and submit to the changes. It's not hard to find illustrations to support this. But even successful transitions are dubious victories because they are often at the price of severed communication with the new Christian's former peer group.

This is hard to admit, but the secularized person who comes to Christ often has no place to go. He and many of our existing churches are worlds apart culturally. This is even more true of those unreached people of the world who live in totally different cultures.

Apparently, I'm not alone in this conclusion. In *Let The Earth Hear His Voice,* Ralph Winter asks, "Are we in America . . . prepared for the fact that most non-Christians yet to be won to Christ (even in our country) will not fit readily into the kinds of churches we now have?"[1]

There are several reasons why this distance between the church and the world exists. It would be beside the point to go into all of them here. Some of the reasons are positive, others are negative. What does concern us here is the fact that Jesus Christ has sent the church into the world, and for this reason we cannot dare lose touch with those who live in the world.

As Jesus related his ambitions for the church to his father just before his death, he said, "I will remain in the world no longer, but they are still in the world . . . they are not of the world any more than I am of the world. My prayer is not that you take them out of the world but that you protect them from the evil one. . . . As you sent me into the world, I have sent them into the world" (John 17:11, 14-15, 18).

To a large degree our purpose for remaining in the world is for *its* sake, not just our own.

But even as Jesus expressed his will for us, he recognized the dilemma he was thrusting upon us: being *in* the world, but not *of* it. How can a Christian obey the call to "come out from them and be separate" (2 Corinthians 6:17) and at the same time be "sent . . . into the world?" (John 17:18).

The Christian's relationship to the world has been a tension point throughout church history. Over the centuries, as Christians have sought to strike a balance between these two seemingly contradictory commands, we have swung from one extreme to the other, from hermit-like isolation to conformity to the world. But either extreme defeats God's purpose. Conformity to the world obscures the glory of God. Isolation renders the Christian model useless. The value of our congruence of life will be lost to the world if separation becomes isolation. "Neither do people light a lamp and put it under a bowl" (Matthew 5:15).

THE PULL TOWARDS ISOLATION IS UNDERSTANDABLE

The world is a hazardous place! "Be self-controlled and alert. Your enemy . . . prowls . . . looking for someone to devour" (1 Peter 5:8).

Compatability with non-Christians is limited. "What fellowship can light have with darkness? . . . What does a believer have in common with an unbeliever? . . . We are the temple of the living God. . . . Therefore come out from them and be separate" (2 Corinthians 6:14-17).

Certain activities don't fit comfortably any longer. "For you have spent enough time in the past doing what pagans choose to do . . . They think it strange that you do not plunge into the same flood of dissipation" (1 Peter 4:3-4).

All things considered, the prudent thing to do seems to be retreat to a "safe distance." The question is, What constitutes a safe distance?

A few years ago I attended a seminar where the lecturer said, "As a Christian takes his stand, he forces his non-Christian friends and acquaintances to choose. They will either be drawn into the Christian life or they will withdraw. Withdrawal also means loss of friendship. Consequently, there will come a time when the maturing Christian has no real friendships among non-Christians." Another teacher said, "As we become more and more mature, we become less and less effective with the world."

Is this what we mean by a safe distance—to think it is a Christian virtue to have no real friendships with unbelievers? If we do, that is tragic, because such isolation has a destructive effect on a local body of Christians, as well as destroying our communication with the lost. Christians who keep to themselves, who do not experience a continuing influx of people just arriving from the dominion of darkness, soon surround themselves with their own subculture. Receiving no feedback from people fresh from the world, they forget what it's like out there. Peculiar language codes, behavioral patterns, and communication techniques emerge that only have meaning for the insiders. As such, a local body becomes increasingly ingrown. It also becomes stranger and stranger to outsiders. Eventually, communication with the man on the street is impossible.

So what is a safe distance? Jesus answered this question with an intriguing statement in John 17:17. He asked his father (in the context of sending his disciples into the world) to "sanctify [set apart for sacred use or make holy] them by the truth; your word is truth." Fundamentally, sanctification is not a matter of geography [where we are], but of the heart (*who* owns it). A safe distance is maintained as we are constantly being transformed by the renewing of our minds through the truth of God's word. This requires time alone with him, when we are actively submitting our minds to the truth. If this practice is not a part of our lives, or if it is not effective, we are ill-prepared for encounters with non-Christians in the world. In such a case, perhaps isolation would be best after all!

Footnotes:

1. Ralph Winter, "The Highest Priority: Cross-Cultural Evangelism," in *Let The Earth Hear His Voice* (Minneapolis: World Wide Publications, 1975), page 221.

FIFTEEN

MUTUAL FEAR

A barrier to honest relationships

THE CHRISTIAN FEARS the influence of the ungodly. On one hand, this is legitimate. "Bad company corrupts good character" (1 Corinthians 15:33). On the other hand, it is not. This kind of fear is mutual. It is also true that the non-Christian fears the Christian, and his fear is also predictable. "For we are to God the aroma of Christ among those who are being saved and those who are perishing. To the one we are the smell of death; to the other, the fragrance of life" (2 Corinthians 2:15-16). The presence of the Christian is a reminder of God's impending judgment. Some of the non-Christian's fears are real; some are groundless.

But whether fears are real or unnecessary, they constitute a formidable blockade against the communication of the gospel. Think for a moment. If you were absolutely free from any fear, what kind of witness would you be?

Even the intrepid apostle Paul had to deal with fear. He

told the Corinthian Christians that he came to them "in weakness and fear, and with much trembling" (1 Corinthians 2:3). He asked the Ephesians for prayer that he would "fearlessly make known the mystery of the gospel" (Ephesians 6:19). Paul's fears were based on past experiences with whips, prisons, and stones. Our fears are more abstract, but not groundless.

The non-Christian fears in part because we are a reminder to him of facts he prefers not to think about: sin, death, and judgment. But some of his fears are due to the censure we transmit to him. These are unjust, because we are not his judge.

OVERCOMING THE NON-CHRISTIAN'S FEARS

The Christian tends to measure the non-Christian against a rather ad hoc list of acceptable and unacceptable behavior. The list is a mixture of clear-cut commands from the word of God such as "do not commit adultery," to relative issues which come from our traditions, such as total abstinence.

The non-Christian picks up the vibrations and feels he is judged. He sometimes even apologizes for his unacceptable habits, indicating that he feels he has fallen into the hands of someone bent on reforming him. Where there are such judgments, communication is hopeless.

But how do we get around this? How do we relate to someone whose sin is destroying himself and those about him? Do we close our eyes when we are with someone who may be brutalizing his family by his infidelities? Can we hide the censure we feel toward him? What is the solution?

Look at Jesus. Jesus managed to accept the worst of us. How? It was because he was a realist. He knew man's capacity for evil, so that was all he expected from him. He also knew man's worst actions are only symptoms of something deeper, and uglier: rebellion against God. It is rebellion, not ignorance, that keeps man from God. And this rebellion is the source of all man's problems. Jesus didn't spend much time treating symptoms. He went for the cure.

This ability to see beyond the surface symptom to the true need is the key to establishing honest relationships with non-Christians. We do not have to condone their behavior to accept and love them.

I have a friend who, when I met him, lived in what was then described as the counter culture. He worked very little and was on drugs. He was not married to the girl he was living with. We began studying the Bible together, but since time was short for me, I invited him to join a study group with several others. These, too, were on their way toward Christ, but the others were a bit more straight, and many were more philosophical than my friend. Consequently, much of what we discussed went right past him.

Finally, during one study, he exploded. "You don't know where I'm coming from! What goes on here doesn't speak to me!"

I agreed. I did not understand him. In response, with a challenging attitude, he invited me to visit his world. We set a date for the next week to spend the evening where his friends gathered. I was in for an education!

We were the first to arrive. Gradually, the place filled up. Each individual was a lesson in himself. Finally the leader strode in. He was fastidiously unkempt, had very long hair, and a beard, and his front teeth were missing. As he sat down he announced, "I quit my job today." By the response of the others, I realized he had just performed the most prestigious action within their structure: quitting one's job. It meant keeping loose, avoiding enduring commitments, letting society pick up the tab.

As his story unfolded I discovered how he had earned the number one ranking among his peers. A university graduate with a military career, he had suddenly left his wife and a job at the Pentagon just to follow his whims. He pushed drugs to sustain an undemanding lifestyle. All he owned was a black pickup truck, a pair of skis, and two large dogs. It was a lifestyle which avoided profound thinking and reflection, preferring what felt good at the moment.

Instructed by the experience, I took my friend out of the Bible study group with the others, and together we studied the Bible in his apartment. His friends, knowing what was happening, would drop around. Occasionally they would take his Bible and read it for themselves. His girlfriend became interested, sat in, and did not miss a word!

But what about dealing with his sin? After he came to Christ we began to work on clearing up its symptoms. The first problem we dealt with was his lack of commitment to his girlfriend.

Thankfully, the laws of God are rational. They are not mindless or arbitrary. By that I mean that if a person existed who possessed all wisdom, and he could answer the question, What are the guidelines for the survival of a society and what must its value system be for it to thrive? I believe the answer would be the Ten Commandments.

What the Bible says about adultery and marriage is not unreasonable. So one day when my friend and I were together, I casually described what I imagined the relationship between the two of them was like—that they really liked each other, that neither wanted to lose the other, but that both knew that no commitments existed on either side. Consequently, they would pretend to a harmony they didn't really feel.

Then I made a projection about the future of their relationship. I told him that eventually the relationship would become a charade as they continued to feign loving responses to each other. Therefore, their relationship was destined to disintegrate under its first real crisis. When the blowup came, both parties would go their way—both very hurt. I then went on to explain how God intends to join man and woman in an inseparable union (Matthew 19:6). This is because any human relationship, if it is to survive, must be based on a mutual commitment.

My friend didn't say a word, but two weeks later we received a wedding invitation. Today they are walking with Christ.

We need to accept the non-Christian as he is, go for the cure, and *then* help him pick his way through the things that are destroying him. Whenever we get this sequence turned around, we become reformers rather than offerers of true healing.

DEALING WITH OUR OWN FEARS

It's our move. If we are going to break the deadlock of isolation, it is obviously up to us. Jesus gave us some simple, easy things to do to help us avoid isolation and be light where it will do the most good—right in the middle of this world's darkness.

In Matthew 5:43-48, he said we should be like our Father who causes the sun to rise on the evil and on the good. He said, Don't just love those who love you back. Even tax collectors do that. Don't just greet your brothers. Everyone does that. Take the initiative in being friendly, and in observing what is happening among those around you.

That isn't very difficult, is it?

In Luke 14:12-13, Jesus suggests that when we give a dinner we shouldn't invite just our friends and relatives. You know how that goes. This time it's our turn, next time it's theirs. In the end, everyone breaks even. It hasn't cost anyone anything. Rather, he says, invite the poor, the crippled, the lame, and the blind who cannot repay you—until the day of resurrection when they will be there to salute your faithfulness to them.

In other words, be hospitable. Deliberately break out of your daily routine of people and places for the gospel's sake. I know of no more effective environment for initiating evangelism than a dinner at home or in a quiet restaurant.

That's not too hard either, is it? We must go into the world to establish the rapport needed to draw people into our lives.

SIXTEEN

WHO ADAPTS TO WHOM?

Making the other person comfortable

CLOSING THE COMMUNICATION gap between Christians and the secularized must become a primary concern if we are to go beyond evangelizing our own kind. Because this need is so basic, I devoted the previous six chapters to the problem.

A short passage by Paul in 1 Corinthians 9 synthesizes this as a single principle. The subject of the passage is clearly evangelism. Paul wrote:

> Though I am free and belong to no man, I make myself a slave to everyone, to win as many as possible. To the Jews I became like a Jew, to win the Jews. To those under the law I became like one under the law (though I myself am not under the law), so as to win those under the law. To those not having the law I became like one not having the law . . . so as to win those not having the law. To the weak I became weak, to win the weak. I have become all things to all men so that by

all possible means I might save some. I do all this for the sake of the gospel, that I may share in its blessings (1 Corinthians 9:19-23).

Paul said that as a witness he recognized it was up to him to adapt to the unevangelized. *The witness adjusts to those he evangelizes,* and not vice versa. Paul defended his freedom to be all things to all men because he knew that was the balance between being "in the world" and being "separate" from it. To be in the world one has to be free to participate in the lives of those around him. Being separate means we do this without compromising the sovereign rule of God in our heart—without sinning, in other words.

What does being "all things to all men" mean in practice? What did it mean for Paul to live like a Jew while among Jews, and then change and live like one without the law when he was among the Gentiles? It meant he would respect the scruples and traditions of whomever he was with, and have the flexibility to set one group's practices aside as he entered the world of persons with different customs.

This struck many as a scandalous thought, but Paul was willing to pay a price for his position. He was a controversial figure among Christians and non-Christians until the day he died. It takes maturity and courage to "go to the Gentiles."

As we discussed why a team of missionaries in his country was having difficulty establishing a solid ministry, a South American said, "Their sanctification is American. I get the impression they are afraid to adapt to the culture because in so doing they would become soiled by the world. They fear they would be 'going pagan.'"

Change *is* hard to face, especially in areas of behavior. Going into the world requires change. It implies participation in people's lives. It means to think, to feel, to understand, and to take seriously the values of those we seek to win.

The incarnation is our prototype. Jesus set his glory aside, "made himself nothing . . . in human likeness . . . he humbled himself" (Philippians 2:7-8). Consequently, "we have one who has been tempted in every way, just as we are—yet was without sin" (Hebrews 4:15). He came into the world, lived life in our presence, and participated with us in life as we live it. He drew the line only at sin. To what degree could we identify with God if there had been no incarnation?

The apostle Paul followed the same principle. He went to non-Christians in order to bring them to God, but he knew their route to God had to pass through his own life. "You are witnesses," he reminded the Thessalonians, "of how holy, righteous and blameless we were among you" (1 Thessalonians 2:10).

For better or for worse, the life a Christian lives in the presence of those he seeks to win is a preview of what the non-Christian's life will become if he accepts what he is hearing. Generally, he will decide either to accept or reject Christianity according to what he has seen. I stumbled onto this rather unnerving truth unwittingly.

A Brazilian friend, Mario, and I studied the Bible for four years together before he became a Christian. As an intellectual who had read almost all of the leading Western thinkers from Rousseau to Kafka, he had blended together a personal philosophy that was fundamentally Marxist—with Bertrand Russell as his patron saint. He was a political activist, a leader in many Marxist activities. Why he kept studying the Bible with me for four years, or why I stuck with him so long, neither of us can explain today. But there we were.

Since he lived life on the philosophical plane, our Bible studies were often pitched in that direction. One day, a couple of years after Mario had become a Christian, he and I were reminiscing. He asked me, "Do you know what it really was that made me decide to become a Christian?" Of course, I immediately thought of our numerous hours of Bible study, but I responded, "No, what?"

His reply took me completely by surprise. He said, "Remember that first time I stopped by your house? We were on our way someplace together and I had a bowl of soup with you and your family. As I sat there observing you, your wife, your children, and how you related to each other, I asked myself, When will I have a relationship like this with my fiancee? When I realized the answer was 'never,' I concluded I had to become a Christian for the sake of my own survival."

I remembered the occasion well enough to recall that our children were not particularly well-behaved that evening. In fact, I remembered I had felt frustrated when I corrected them in Mario's presence.

Mario saw that Christianity binds a family together. The last verse in the Old Testament refers to turning "the hearts of the fathers to their children, and the hearts of the children to their fathers" (Malachi 4:6).

Our family was unaware of our influence on Mario. God had done this work through our family without our knowing it. Most Christians are probably unaware of most of the improvements God makes on us in the sanctification process.

We tend to see the weaknesses and incongruities in our lives, and our reaction is to recoil at the thought of letting outsiders get close enough to see us as we really are. Even if our assessment is accurate, it is my observation that any Christian who is sincerely seeking to walk with God, in spite of all his flaws, reflects something of Christ. It seems that the better we think we are doing, the worse we come across.

SUMMARY

It is not enough, then, to occasionally drop into another individual's world, preach to him, and go our way. Somehow, he needs to be brought into our world as well. If he isn't, the view he gets of us is so fragmented he could miss the total picture. He doesn't see the effects the grace of God has had in our day-to-day lives.

But this two-way interaction will never happen unless we Christians learn how to become "all things to all men."

SEVENTEEN

THE WITNESS OF THE BODY

Supplementing each other's abilities

FROM THE BEGINNING, one of God's primary means of revealing himself to the world has been through a people, as we have seen. First, there was Israel, the nation that moved from slavery to incomparable beauty in a few generations. Then God raised up the church, turning a bewildered group of 120 disciples cloistered in a Jerusalem room into a unique people whose very existence placed the world in check.

God has always used a people to amplify his voice in the world—and he always will. This fact has major significance for both our concept of evangelism and how we witness.

In practical terms, what *does* this mean? There are two major implications. First, there is the corporate testimony; second, there is the body principle.

THE CORPORATE TESTIMONY
In his book, *The Church at the End of the Twentieth Century,*

Francis Schaeffer observes, "The church is to be a loving church in a dying culture. How then is the dying culture going to consider us? Jesus said, 'By this shall all men know that ye are my disciples, if ye have love one to another.' In the midst of the world, in the midst of our present dying culture, Jesus is giving a right to the world. Upon his authority, he gives the world the right to judge whether you and I are born-again Christians on the basis of our observable love toward all Christians."[1]

Jesus prayed, "that all of them may be one, Father . . . so that the world may believe that you have sent me" (John 17:21). In commenting on this verse, Schaeffer writes, "Here Jesus is stating . . . we cannot expect the world to believe that the Father sent the Son, that Jesus' claims are true, and that Christianity is true, unless the world sees some reality of the oneness of true Christians."[2]

The Christian who seeks to win the lost while operating alone or separated from other believers is deprived of a critical resource. Even though he may clearly demonstrate the fruit of the Spirit, those he seeks to win often do not feel the full impact of his witness, just because he is alone. It's so easy to discount or explain away an isolated individual: "He has an unusual background," or, "he's strange." But when faced with a body of believers, the common denominator—the Holy Spirit—quickly stands out. Then their corporate testimony is irrefutable.

Sometimes working alone is unavoidable. For example, working alone, or as a small team, is inherent in the work of an apostle who goes to places or peoples where no Christian community exists. Paul said, "It has always been my ambition to preach the gospel where Christ was not known, so that I would not be building on someone else's foundation" (Romans 15:20).

This apostolic or missionary function is still an essential element in the church because the world is still full of peoples and subcultures which do not have a Christian base. I am living in such a subculture as I write this.

It is an excruciating experience to start from scratch. Those first contacts are usually hard to come by. Finally there are a few, scattered here and there about town. But they may not even know one another, and have no sense of unity. But soon they begin to demonstrate a desire to see their friends and families come to know Christ. Often this desire is present from the very first days of their spiritual life. I wonder if this isn't something God plants early in the heart of a new Christian to make him aware of his dependence on others. As a new Christian begins sharing the good news with others, he becomes aware of his need to learn more effective ways of presenting the message. The desire to meet this felt need is one of the major gravitational pulls that draws new Christians together and into relationships with more mature believers.

This was another of those discoveries I stumbled on through experience, only later discovering its biblical origins.

Several years ago a colaborer and I found ourselves in a nucleus of new Christians who needed and wanted to learn how to communicate the gospel to their peers. But they were in no way equipped to do this themselves. Most of them had never even picked up a Bible before we met them. How could we help them to influence their friends effectively?

Often, when faced with such a situation, the Christian worker takes it on himself to go and talk to the friend. This is generally an opportunity lost, for when it happens, the new Christian quickly draws an erroneous conclusion: that evangelism is for the professionals only. When the Christian worker goes out to make such a visit, the new Christian heads for the sidelines where he sits for the remainder of his Christian life.

We had to avoid that! But how could we lead a group of new Christians who know so little into effective evangelism?

In seeking an answer we came up with what we called "the open study." The open study is a series of six weekly or fortnightly studies geared for non-Christians. It is conducted in a neutral, personal environment, usually in someone's home. There is an informal atmosphere—samba music and coffee. A short, provocative presentation on some facet of the Christian message is given, such as Who is Jesus Christ? or What is man? This is followed by a free-for-all discussion where *any* question is welcomed. To keep it alive, we make sure half the group are non-Christians and half are Christians.

To get the most out of the open studies as a training experience, we would coach one of our new Christians and help him prepare to lead the discussion. Christians who attended were instructed to avoid giving those suffocating pat answers Christians are capable of.

The open study was a success—such a success that one day Osvaldo came to me and said, "I've decided not to bring any more of my friends to these open studies. Everyone who comes ends up becoming a Christian. I feel the studies are becoming a crutch for me. I'm not learning to evangelize a person on my own."

I didn't know how to respond to Osvaldo, but I began to observe more closely what was happening. What made the open study so effective? It couldn't have been content, for often the presentations were quite weak. And it wasn't the discussions. My colleague and I had resolved to keep mostly silent. Many times that was painful as we watched the non-Christians massacre our offspring. But I began to hear one comment over and over again from the guests: "I've never seen people like this before—they are different from any I've ever been with." Finally, after frequent repetition, the message got through. People were responding in the open studies not primarily to what they were *hearing*, but to what they were *seeing*. They had never seen a group or a nucleus of Christians before.

Then some more thoughts began to fall into place. Where did Osvaldo get the idea that he should be able to carry on the evangelization of his friends singlehandedly? Undoubtedly, from me! And where did I get that idea from?

God never intended evangelism to be an individualistic effort. The biblical pattern is for the individual's witness to be carried on within the setting of a corporate effort. The corporate witness says, "Look at all of us. This is what you too can become. There's hope." It's possible to discount or explain away an isolated individual, but it's impossible to refute the corporate testimony. The apostle John observed, "No one has ever seen God; but if we love each other, God lives in us and his love is made complete in us" (1 John 4:12).

THE BODY PRINCIPLE

Evangelism tends to assume one of two forms: either mass proclamation, or personal witness. Both of these are good, but they represent only a fraction of what really should be taking place. Both approaches tend to exclude most Christians. Mass proclamation can easily deprive the individual of his responsibility to develop as a witness, while on the other hand, when it comes to personal evangelism, the Christian is usually left to learn by himself. And many Christians do not feel gifted for personal witnessing.

When it comes to winning the lost, more often than not we distribute a few tools, occasionally conduct a short-lived evangelistic assault, exhort, and generally leave everyone with a guilty conscience. Isn't there some way for the average Christian to be involved in evangelism in a more enduring, more realistic manner?

The one overriding truth in the New Testament regarding the church is the fact that it is a body, a living organism whose members must exist in a constant state of interdependence. (See 1 Corinthians 12, Ephesians 4, and Romans 12.) If this truth needs to be applied anywhere, it is in this matter of evangelism.

Much has been written and taught about discovering and exercising one's spiritual gifts. Generally the question, What is my gift? is a difficult one. On what basis can I answer? It is better to ask, What can I *do?* Everyone can answer that. It is in doing what we are able to do that we can answer the first question. We will discover our gifts in action!

How often have you heard someone say, "Evangelism isn't my gift"? Technically, there is no such thing. No one possesses the gift of evangelism. Some, however, possess gifts that make them especially effective in evangelism. 1 Corinthians 12:4-6 describes different kinds of services *and* different kinds of gifts.

When we begin to look at evangelism as a corporate ministry, we soon discover that virtually any spiritual gift that builds up the body, also has its place in winning the lost. That is because we cannot separate winning the lost from edifying the body. One cannot exist without the other. Evangelism as a function of the body takes place when a handful of disciples band together, and pool their abilities and resources for the sake of reaching into the world with their message. Under these circumstances, whatever gifts are represented can be put to good use. Whatever comes naturally for you—hospitality, the ability to organize, gregariousness, the ability to pray, cooking, Bible knowledge, teaching—whatever you can do can be useful in evangelism. Your gift—your abilities, strengths, and interests—can build up the body and also build bridges of communication to non-Christians. Start with what you have. As you go along, you will acquire abilities you do not now possess.

A few years ago, five engineers graduated in the same class from the University of Curitiba in Brazil. All were young Christians of varying degrees of maturity. Together they decided to move to the city of Sao Paulo for the sake of the kingdom of God.

Sao Paulo is a city of fourteen million with a minimal Christian presence. It is one of the neediest cities on earth. None of the five had found jobs when they moved into an apartment together. They pooled their money. It ran out. Finally, as they were beginning literally to go hungry, one of them found a job. He was the youngest Christian of them all. Six weeks had gone by. The five began living off his salary. Eleven months later the last of the five, Evilasio, found employment. He was the most mature Christian of them all, the one whose faith spearheaded the venture.

None of these men knew much about evangelism. None

were experienced leaders or Bible teachers, but the little they had learned, when pooled together, was enough. They planted the gospel among their new acquaintances and colleagues. A new body of believers was born.

Ephesians 4:11-12 clearly indicates that the function of the leaders (the apostles, prophets, evangelists, pastors, and teachers) is to prepare God's people for the ministry. We need to understand that the ministry is every Christian's responsibility. There are to be no spectators because whatever gifts one has are important when used jointly with other gifts. Then we begin to see things happen that are otherwise impossible. Evangelism is not limited to those who specialize in the proclamation of the Gospel. We accomplish together things we can never hope for when operating alone.

Probably the most simple, reproducible application of what we've been talking about is the neighborhood Bible study. What's required? It calls for being an observant, thoughtful neighbor. It means making a home available. It involves inviting people and knowing their interests and needs. It means being willing to lead a Bible discussion. Someone needs to feel responsible for holding such a group together and keeping it moving. When it gets too big, someone needs to realize it is time to divide and start a new outreach group. And that's about it! Imagine what would happen if all of us were involved in an effort of this sort.

What we just described is close to the basic form available to the church for the first three hundred years of its history. Persecuted, the Christians could not operate openly. There were no church buildings. They depended on homes and other structures (see Romans 15 and 16). I wonder if the church didn't lose something essential to its nature when we extracted it from our living rooms and shops and began to house it in specially designed buildings. Gone was the insatiable demand for leadership development that those networks of cells produced. As routines became more established, the pressure of responsibility was lifted from the average Christian. But we need those pressures. The church is intended to be more like a guerrilla force than a fixed fortification.

CONCLUSION

We are individually responsible before God to use whatever abilities and resources we have to win the lost. But this does not mean evangelism is to be an individual exercise. Evangelism is also a group effort. Few of us can fulfill our part in this ministry unless we band together, and pool our resources with a few kindred spirits to accomplish the common objective of witnessing as a body of believers by actively participating in the lives of some non-Christian friends.

Footnotes:
1. Francis Schaeffer, *The Church at the End of the Twentieth Century* (Downers Grove, Illinois: Inter-Varsity Press, 1970), pages 136-137.
2. Ibid., pages 138-139.

EIGHTEEN

THREE SIMULTANEOUS INFLUENCES

Life, body, and verbal witness

WE CAN EXPECT God to use us in three ways as part of his work of reconciling people to himself:

Through the witness of our lives
Through the witness of the body
Through the verbal witness

THE WITNESS OF THE LIFE

We have already observed that to witness with our lives is to incarnate the gospel by the way we live. Our life is to be like Christ's in our dealings with others—full of grace and truth. It means being redemptive in our relationships.

Twenty years ago I heard Dr. Bob Smith, a godly, beloved professor at Bethel College in St. Paul, Minnesota, make a casual comment that has since made a permanent mark on me. He had just returned from two years of teaching in the Middle East and his mind was fresh with experiences of involvement with Muslims. He described how the people grasped at whatever display of personal interest or friendliness he would show them. Then he said, "You know, 90 percent of evangelism is love."

I didn't know that! In fact, at the time, as a hungry young Christian bent on achieving, I saw evangelism simply as an activity I engaged in. The people involved were more like objects needing saving, rather than real persons. I was after results, with no time to waste on loving anybody.

But Dr. Smith was right. The apostle Paul said, "Christ's love compels us, because we are convinced that one died for all" (2 Corinthians 5:14). Notice the origin of this love that motivated Paul. It was Christ's love. Christ's love, in turn, reflected the Father's love. God started it. "We love because he first loved us" (1 John 4:19). This is the witness of a life.

I have to admit I never saw much enduring fruit in evangelism until I began to understand the importance of this truth and began to put it into practice.

THE WITNESS OF THE BODY

We have also considered the collective impact a nucleus of Christians can have on the non-Christian. The simple fact that the group exists, with its unique ability to love one another, is in itself a powerful statement to the world. It is a testimony to the reality of our message: that we are, in fact, a transformed people; that Jesus was truly sent by the Father; and that there is hope for anybody.

But if we expect this testimony to be heard and heeded, the members of the body of Christ need to see themselves as being *in* in the world, *for the sake of the world.* This is the witness of the body.

THE VERBAL WITNESS

If our witness should end with the first two, however, it would be incomplete. "How can they believe the one of whom they have not heard? And how can they hear without someone preaching to them? . . . 'How beautiful are the feet of those who bring good news'" (Romans 10:14-15).

What people see must be verbally interpreted before the communication circle is closed. "How can I [understand] . . . unless someone explains it to me?" the Ethiopian asked Phillip (Acts 8:31). We must talk about our faith.

DOING THREE THINGS AT ONCE

It would be easy to get the impression that I am suggesting a sequence—that it's necessary to devote a period of time to establishing a personal friendship, so that eventually the person can be brought around to meet our Christian friends, so that finally we can say something to him. If I left you with this impression, I would lead you into a non-productive trap.

Because we can expect God to use us in all three ways *at the same time,* these three influences—our lives, the band of kindred spirits of which we are a part, and our words—should all be *sustained* until the person we are seeking to reach encounters Christ and moves into discipleship.

Any one of these influences, by itself, is incomplete. The defects of a silent witness are obvious, but an exclusively verbal witness is also seriously defective. An exclusively verbal witness is impersonal, even when carried on at an individual level. In 1 Thessalonians 2:8 Paul wrote, "We loved you so much that we were delighted to share with you not only the gospel of God but our lives as well, because you had become so dear to us."

So all three influences work together. Which comes first varies with the situation, but it has been my experience that I need to talk about my faith early in a relationship. I've found that the longer I wait, the more difficult it becomes. Patterns develop in the friendship that are hard to break out of later. We don't have to say much at the outset; often just enough to "get the flag up" will suffice.

When the verbal witness comes first, the other two influences need to be brought in as soon as possible.

Larry was a secularized individual, a fringe counter-culture existentialist. We had just moved to a different city in the

United States and I made his acquaintance at a party we attended soon after arriving.

As we chatted together I explained that I was new in town and, therefore, had few acquaintances. I told him I customarily met with a few friends to examine the Bible, and since I was not yet doing that, it was something I missed. I said he would be doing me a favor by joining me. He replied that he didn't believe in God and knew nothing about the Bible, but if he could help me, he would be happy to try. He was my favorite kind of person, and I told him so. We set a time to meet again.

We started out as strangers studying the Bible, but soon we developed a close, yet informal social relationship as we played tennis, skied, and ate meals together. Meanwhile, I had gathered together a few more friends and acquaintances who joined us.

Larry struggled with the content and claims of the gospel. He had many honest intellectual problems, as well as the customary battles with the will. It is when these inner battles begin that the importance of love in a relationship becomes crucial. The natural reaction for the non-Christian at this point is to flee the message—to go anywhere but near that Bible again! But mutual love, and friendship within a small circle of friends holds him. The Holy Spirit uses these influences to sustain the non-Christian's exposure to the Scriptures.

This is what happened to Larry. These three influences—the witness of a life, the witness of the body, and a verbal witness—worked together until it became apparent he had become a Christian. In his case the initial point of contact was a verbal witness.

BECOMING VERBAL

"But in your hearts set apart Christ as Lord. Always be prepared to give an answer to everyone who asks you to give the reason for the hope that you have" (1 Peter 3:15). "Be wise in the way you act towards outsiders, make the most of every opportunity. Let your conversation be always full of grace,

seasoned with salt, so that you may *know how to answer*
(Colossians 4:5-6).

If our lives reflect Jesus Christ, that quality will not go
unobserved. Questions will be directed our way as our friends
and acquaintances try to fathom what they see in us. But
usually such questions come indirectly and are veiled. Seldom
does anyone ask, "Why are you the way you are"?

Instead, the question is expressed in the form of a com-
plaint against a spouse, or in an expression of worry over un-
controllable children. Or it can be an expression of disillusionment, cynicism, or feelings of futility. Sometimes the riding
you take for your faith is nothing more than an awkward attempt to get you to open up!

Therefore we need to learn not just how to give answers,
but to recognize these indirect questions. We need to learn to
listen. At first we miss most of the questions that come our
way, or they dawn on us an hour or a day later, when it's too
late. Then we kick ourselves for being so insensitive.

Dawson Trotman, founder of The Navigators, observed
that it is impossible to always have an answer ready for any
question that may come our way. That is understandable. But,
he would say, we should not allow ourselves to be caught a
second time by the same question. In other words, when we
miss an opportunity, or handle one poorly, we should reflect
on what happened and rehearse to ourselves what we *should*
have said and what *should* have taken place in that situation. If
we do not know how to respond properly, we should search
for the correct answer.

You will be amazed at the difference this exercise will
make in your effectiveness in fulfilling the commands of
1 Peter 3:15 and Colossians 4:5, 6.

DON'T SAY TOO MUCH

We are given to extremes. Either we say nothing and let an opportunity slip past us, or we say too much and drive people
away.

It is not always right or convenient to take the time

necessary to explain the entire message. Better to say just enough to prepare the way for a more propitious occasion, like a lunch or dinner date.

And what about the young Christian, or those who are not able to express themselves well? How are they going to verbalize the message? It doesn't take much. All the Samaritan woman knew to say was, "Come, see a man who told me everything I ever did. Could this be the Christ?" (John 4:29).

Andrew went to his brother Simon Peter and said, "We have found the Messiah" (John 1:41) and then brought Peter to Jesus.

Philip went to his friend Nathanael and said, "We have found the one Moses wrote about . . . Jesus of Nazareth" (John 1:45). Nathanael complicated things by saying, "Nazareth! Can anything good come from there?" But Philip responded with a simple, "Come and see" (John 1:46).

We have found Jesus, come and see. Winsome words, easy enough for anyone to use. Often saying any more complicates rather than enhances our efforts.

NINETEEN

THE BIBLICAL BASIS FOR FAITH

Conscious submission to God through his word

OUR OBJECTIVE IN witnessing is to bring people to faith in Jesus Christ. Mark Twain defined faith as "believing in something you know really isn't true." But a valid faith is just the opposite—it *must* be based on truth.

One of the most helpful definitions of faith in the Bible is found in Romans 4:21: "being fully persuaded that God had power to do what he had promised." Faith is the confidence that God will do what he has said he will do. Coming to faith then, means *knowing* what God has said and done, and then staking one's life on it. Faith in God is not a leap in the dark. It is a conscious, voluntary submission to his will for us.

Evangelism provides the non-Christian with the kind of input he needs to respond to God on the level of faith. For this we need to lay a base of truth. At what point can we know that has been accomplished? It is not always easy to evaluate.

In an unpublished paper on "The Doctrine of Sin in

Cross-cultural Church Planting,'' Wayne Dye described the efforts of a group of missionaries working among New Guinea highlanders. As they involved themselves with these primitive people, the missionaries became extremely concerned with the polygamy and betel-nut chewing they observed among the villagers—so much so that these two practices became the watershed issues for Christian fellowship.

The villagers, however, felt other issues were more serious. To them, a long life depended more upon the avoidance of discord.

Dye reported one case where a number of converts had responded to the missionaries' efforts. They were baptized and for several years they tithed, attended church, and obeyed the imported rules for Christian behavior. One day the village leaders went to the missionaries and said, "We ought to have done enough by now to repay Jesus for his death." Then they reverted to paganism.

What happened? Faith had not occurred at all. Something that *looked* like Christian faith had been constructed upon the highlander's pagan presuppositions. Consequently, the villagers had gone along with the missionaries until they tired of it, and then went their own way.

In a case like this where the contrast is so sharp between Christianity and paganism, it doesn't require unusual perception to recognize what went wrong. But this same danger lurks wherever evangelism occurs, and it is often very difficult to spot.

I met Henrique in Curitiba, Brazil, in January, 1964. We met in an art store and struck up a conversation.

Henrique was one of the most brilliant men I have known. He was a voracious reader with a retentive memory. He could discuss any subject from Byzantine art to the genetic code as if he had finished a book on the subject the day before. Along with Portuguese, he spoke flawless English and Spanish. He also spoke German and French. He was twenty-one when we met, recently married, and the owner of a language school.

Henrique and I drifted from the art store over to a restaurant where we had tea together. His first question was, "What are you, an American, doing in Curitiba?" When I told him, he replied, "Fine, convert me first, then we'll have a whole school we can go to work on." He meant it. He wanted me to explain the gospel right there, and he had decided to accept it even before he had heard what I had to say. I held him off until the next day so we could sit down and work our way through the Bible together. That next day Henrique made a decision. A few weeks later his wife followed suit. He and I saw each other every day for several years. A deep friendship developed. We became like brothers.

But I had known Henrique only a week or so when I spotted a dangerous weakness. I noticed it the first time we ate a meal together. He was uncontrolled in his eating. Alerted, I began watching for other symptoms of lack of self-control. They were present in the way he handled his money, in the way he ran his business, and in the urgency with which he smoked. I was scared. "The fruit of the Spirit is . . . self-control" (Galatians 6:22-23). But it wasn't there.

The Bible was still a novelty to Henrique, so he was busy devouring that. He was an audacious witness, but that too was still a novelty. I knew when the newness wore off and when continued progress had to depend upon a deeper level of motivation, we would be in trouble. We were.

When he ceased to open the Bible on his own, we began to do it together to compensate for his lack of personal discipline. Daily for over two years he and I met over the Scriptures. Consequently, Henrique's life maintained a semblance of Christian behavior. But I never saw the Holy Spirit do anything about his root problems. I grew irritated with God and asked him why I had to do his part of the job as well as my own. That attitude didn't help either.

I couldn't sustain those daily transfusions indefinitely. So after a couple of years had gone by, I decided I had to wean him. Henrique would have to begin getting his nourishment from God himself.

When we returned to Curitiba after being away for a seven-month furlough, we found that Henrique's business had gone bankrupt, and he had divorced his wife, and left town.

The last time Henrique and I were together was in a restaurant in Porto Alegre in 1971. His second career and his second marriage were disintegrating. In the course of our conversation he said, "You don't know how close you came to getting me to become a Christian back there in Curitiba!"

Henrique had been attempting to live the Christian life without being a Christian, and I had been trying to help him. How futile! Henrique had made a decision but I had not helped him lay an adequate basis for faith. Consequently, he and I spent two years perpetuating an illusion.

We must take care that faith is constructed on the only sure foundation, the rock of the living word of God, incarnate and written (see Ephesians 2:20). Faith cannot rest on anything else, without being syncretized with other religious beliefs, or pagan or humanistic presuppositions. We come to God on his terms, not ours.

How easy it is to gloss over big issues with a few glib phrases, elicit a prayer, or some other action we interpret as "a decision," and move on, happy with our success. One of the challenges for the missionary is to discern whether those he is ministering to have actually put their faith in Jesus Christ, or are merely following the missionary himself. Sometimes an entire generation can go by before such a misplaced trust is discovered.

So wherever evangelism takes place, the witness should seek for a genuine response. Superficial, well-meaning decisions tend to sabotage the real thing. In Henrique's case, he had done everything I told him was necessary for conversion. So both he and I assumed a spiritual rebirth had occurred when it actually hadn't. When this happens, the effect will be either confusion, as in our case, or disillusionment.

When a person has tried our offer, and is expecting the promised benefits which never materialize, the end result is likely to be disillusionment. When I shared the gospel with a next-door neighbor while living in the United States, he replied, "Hell, I've been saved three times." He had tried it, but it hadn't worked, so he was into something else.

How do we avoid this?

Three elements of personality are involved in making a decision to become a Christian, or in making any significant decision for that matter. They are the emotions, the intellect, and the will.

For example, a young man meets a young woman. They are immediately attracted to one another. They both say to themselves, "Now there is someone I'd like to marry." At that point, if the emotions had their way, there would be a wedding. But the intellect intervenes, questioning the impulsive emotional response. Would we be compatible? What is she really like? Can I afford to support her? Both conclude it would be better to take some more time and answer a few questions before they proceed. So the two begin spending more time with each other. He eventually concludes that she is as beautiful on the inside as she is on the outside. Now his intellect has sided with the emotions on the idea of marriage.

But the final and heaviest vote remains to be cast—that of the will. It stops the march toward the altar with the question, Am I willing to give up this lifestyle for another? What about my freedom—is it worth the trade? What about the added responsibility—am I willing to assume it? The marriage will occur only when the will finally agrees with the emotions and the intellect. And so it is in coming to Christ.

Isn't this the message of the parable of the sower?

> When anyone hears the message about the kingdom and does not understand it, the evil one comes and snatches away what was sown in his heart. This is the seed sown along the path. What was sown on rocky places is the man who hears the word and at once receives it with joy. But since he has no root, he lasts only a short time. When trouble or persecution

comes because of the word, he quickly falls away. What was sown among thorns is the man who hears the word, but the worries of this life and the deceitfulness of wealth choke it, making it unfruitful. But what was sown on good soil is the man who hears the word and understands it. He produces a crop yielding a hundred, sixty or thirty times what was sown (Matthew 13:19-23).

The difference in the response is in the differences in the soil, not in the seed. Four kinds of soil. Four different responses.

1. *There was the seed sown on the path.* The path was hard. There was not enough loose soil there to produce even an emotional response. We all know people like this. Indifferent, they seem not to care about spiritual things. These are the most difficult of all to attempt to win. Such people may be cultured and gracious, but impervious to the word of God. Their only hope is for God to break up their hardness, thus changing the consistency of the soil, and preparing it to receive the good seed. With people like this, the place to begin is with intercession. God does break up their hardness as we pray. I've seen him do it often, and it's always awesome.

2. *Then there's the rocky soil.* This person hears and initially receives the word with joy. He responds emotionally, but lacks an adequate basis for faith, so his response is short-lived. What happened? These people do their thinking *after* making a decision. They have second thoughts about what they have done and feel embarrassed over their gullibility or impulsiveness. Very often they will avoid those who were responsible for leading them to the decision.

In such situations, the parable explains, there was no real understanding. The intellect has not been satisfied that what was being decided could stand up to closer scrutiny. For some reason, the person just wasn't mentally ready for a binding commitment to Christ.

3. *Some seed falls on the thorny soil.* Here the seed does germinate. It looks good. Surely this time there's life! But

other seeds lie unnoticed in this same soil. They are "the worries of this life," and the "deceitfulness of wealth." They are other concerns and ambitions. The will is harboring other commitments which in time choke off the person's response to the gospel.

Why does a person like this make a decision to become a Christian at all? He may make a decision simply because he has run out of arguments against the gospel. He can no longer come up with any good reasons why he shouldn't become a Christian—even though he really doesn't want to. It's usually not very difficult to destroy a person's arguments against the gospel. Often when someone finds himself in this position, he simply says, "You win." He gives in to the truth, but he doesn't submit his life to Christ. His will remains intact.

Have you ever stopped to reflect on how easy it would be for God to prove his existence to every breathing soul? Or take Jesus—why didn't he go back to the temple in Jerusalem just one time after he rose from the dead to give just one discourse, and personally confront those who had killed him three days earlier? Instead of doing that, he limited himself to visiting those who already believed. Had he returned to the temple, the whole world would have acknowledged his Messiahship. Why didn't he do it? I believe it was because he wasn't interested in the kind of response such an act would have encouraged. The world would have capitulated to his sovereignty against its will. There would have been no faith, no love, just a grudging admission as to the truth of his message.

The day will come when what I have just described will happen, but it will be the day of judgment.

Another reason a person will make a decision to become a Christian, while at the same time insisting on keeping his own will intact, is that he thinks he can make it work that way. But he can't. We come to God on his terms or not at all.

Jesus went through a phase of popularity in his three-and-one-half years of ministry. Masses of people followed him everywhere. They liked what he had to say. They were fascinated by his miracles. They wanted to make him king. Judging by outward appearances, Jesus was highly successful. But rather than being impressed by the response, he deliberately stung the multitude with a series of very hard statements that offended them and drove them back to their homes (see John 6:25-66).

What was the issue? The people were following him for the wrong reasons. He told them that unless they were prepared to accept him as the only source of eternal life, they had nothing in common with him. Although they liked Jesus, they weren't ready to give him a central place in their lives. Offended by his demands, they went their way.

The will has always been the greatest hindrance to personal faith. That is because man's basic problem ever since the Fall has been rebellion. Satan told Eve, "You will be like God" (Genesis 3:5). That was an attractive offer! Rebellion is insisting on being one's own god (see Isaiah 53:6).

God is limited in what he can do with a rebellious individual. He created us in such a way that he cannot violate our freedom of choice. This fact is reflected in an appeal God made to his people: "Why will you die, O house of Israel? For I take no pleasure in the death of anyone. . . . Repent and live" (Ezekiel 18:31-32).

Often we evangelize those around us as if ignorance were the main obstacle to faith. It is an obstacle, but a secondary one. Imagine how easy it would be to evangelize your city if the task merely involved informing the ignorant! But salvation means submission to Christ. There can be no other way.

4. *The fourth soil is the good soil.* "It is the man who hears the word and understands it." We know he's good soil because he's fruitful. Where there's fruit, we know there's life.

How do we know when spiritual life has been created? How do we know when a baby has been born? Life speaks for itself. Becoming a Christian is equivalent to receiving the Holy Spirit (see Romans 8:9). Can it be possible for the Creator of all that exists, the one who possesses all power and wisdom, to slip into a life and remain there unnoticed? The proof of spiritual life is not merely in being able to give the right answers to certain questions. It is in the evidence of the fruit of the Spirit: "Love, joy, peace, patience, kindness, goodness, faithfulness, gentleness and self-control" (Galatians 5:22-23).

Assurance of salvation for the young Christian comes from the same source. "This is how we know that he lives in us: We know it by the Spirit he gave us" (1 John 3:24).

TWENTY

THE DYNAMICS OF CONVERSION

The Christian, the Holy Spirit, and the Scriptures

WE HAVE CONCLUDED that the basic obstacle to faith is rebellion, not ignorance. If this is true, the means God uses to draw man to himself will bear it out. As we saw earlier, God influences nations, and works through circumstances and events to prepare people for his message. Beyond this, God has other influences at his disposal: the Holy Spirit, the Scriptures, and the Christian. These are the three basic means God uses in his work of reconciliation.

We have already discussed how God employs the Christian on three levels—through the witness of his life, through the collective witness of Christians, and through each one's verbal witness. In this chapter we will examine the other two influences; the Holy Spirit, and the Scriptures.

THE HOLY SPIRIT

The need to get something going was almost overwhelming as

we began our ministry in Curitiba, Brazil, in 1964. There we were with all the trappings family living implies. On one occasion, at the height of my frustration, I wrote in my journal, "I am a full-fledged missionary now. I have a house, a car, and a camera. The only thing missing is a ministry."

We were foreigners, strangers in town, and didn't know a soul. I found myself casting about for something I could do, some activity that would justify my existence to myself.

I soon discovered it's not hard to find things to do if you are not choosy. Opportunities began opening up, but as I considered them, God convicted me with an unsettling thought from Matthew 15:13. It dogged me everywhere I went and still does. Jesus said, "Every plant that my heavenly Father has not planted will be pulled up by the roots."

How simple it is to get into some activity out of a misplaced sense of duty, or because we were asked and couldn't say no, or because it was something we just felt like doing. I realized that if God was not committed to what I got myself into in Curitiba, eventually my efforts would be pulled up by the roots. Nothing would remain. Considering the options, I elected to turn down the opportunities I was contemplating and live with my tensions. God was going to have to make the first move. My dependence on the Holy Spirit reached a new level of desperation. I reviewed some promises in Isaiah 45:13-14. For six months I began every day by opening my Bible to those verses, praying, and claiming those promises for our ministry in Brazil.

Jesus said, "Apart from me you can do nothing" (John 15:5). If the Holy Spirit is not committed in tangible ways to what we are doing, we should find out what's wrong or give it up. After he had risen, Jesus told his disciples to go to Jerusalem and lock themselves in a room to wait for the Holy Spirit to be sent. That was all they were capable of doing until the Holy Spirit arrived on the scene.

THE HOLY SPIRIT IN CONVERSION
In John 16:7-11, Jesus described the role of the Holy Spirit in

the reconciliation process. He said he would send the Holy Spirit to his disciples and that when he came, he would convict the world of guilt in regard to three things: sin, righteousness, and judgment. These are exactly the three things needed to change the consistency of the soil of a person's heart in order for it to receive the good seed, which is the word of God.

Jesus expanded on these three things with three cause-and-effect statements: "In regard to sin, because men do not believe in me; in regard to righteousness, because I am going to the Father . . . and in regard to judgment, because the prince of this world now stands condemned" (John 16:9-11). The cause and effect relationship in these three phrases is not immediately apparent.

What does the Holy Spirit's convicting a person of his sin have to do with not believing in Jesus Christ? It has everything to do with it. Unbelief is the root of all sin. It is synonymous with rebellion. In Luke 16 we read about the rich man, who, finding himself in hell, became concerned about his brothers. So he asked that Lazarus, the beggar who once lived by his front door who also had died, should be sent to his brothers on earth to warn them. Abraham's reply to his request was even more unusual: "They have Moses and the Prophets [the Old Testament]; let them listen to them. . . . If they do not listen to Moses and the Prophets, they will not be convinced even if someone rises from the dead" (Luke 16:29,31).

Here again we are reminded that the basic problem with man is not ignorance, but rebellion. When people don't believe the gospel message when they hear it, it is because they don't want to. So God sends his persuader, the Holy Spirit, to convict man of his sin.

What about the second phrase? Jesus said the Holy Spirit would convict men of guilt "in regard to righteousness," because he was "going to the Father" (John 16:10). What is the relationship here? Simply this: Jesus is the perfect standard of righteousness. His life defined righteousness. While he was physically present in this world, man's unrighteousness was laid bare. This is supported by his statements, "I am the light of the world" and, "You are going to have the light just a little while longer. Walk while you have the light, before darkness overtakes you" (John 12:35). When Jesus left this world, he sent the Holy Spirit to take over this function. Today, the Spirit is the one who measures the dimensions of true righteousness in a person's heart, to show him how far he falls short.

What about the third phrase, "in regard to judgment, because the prince of this world now stands condemned" (John 16:11)? What is the cause and effect relationship here? We live on a fallen planet that is plagued by sin. This whole creation is coming into judgment. Satan, the prince of this world, has been mortally wounded.

Meanwhile the non-Christian lives and acts as if both his achievements and his possessions will somehow last forever. One of the things the Holy Spirit does for the non-Christian is to make him aware of the precariousness, futility, and brevity of his life.

The Holy Spirit convicts of sin, righteousness, and judgment. What a relief to discover that this responsibliity has been assigned to him, rather than to us!

THE SCRIPTURES IN CONVERSION

The Bible is our authority. It is able to stand on its own against the unbeliever. Our job, as witnesses, is not to defend it, but to give it an opportunity to work.

But what do we do with the non-Christian who refuses to accept the authority of the Scriptures? The secularized person's position implies either unbelief or a rejection of the authority of Scripture. Then what?

We should not allow ourselves to get drawn into discussions over the inspiration and authority of the Bible. Not that this is not an important issue, but it's just not the right place to begin. The truths of the gospel have their sequence and we cannot deal with them out of that sequence any more than one could put a roof on a house that hasn't been framed up.

We have a friend, Jorge, who became a Christian. Then his fiancee, Elisa, accepted Christ. Elisa's German father, who was still a loyal supporter of the Third Reich, was aghast. He came to our house to find out who we were and what we were doing with his daughter. He was so angry that as he crossed our living room he didn't see a large wooden coffee table in the middle of the room. He smashed into the table so hard he upset it. In his rage, partly because of what had happened to his daughter and partly because of the pain in his shin, he announced loudly that he was going to begin a study of the Bible from cover to cover to disprove its credibililty. He was going to begin in Genesis and work his way through, and record all the errors and contradictions he discovered.

Of course, he never made it. Every question he raised remained inconclusive. He gave up somewhere in the deserts of Leviticus and Numbers. Meanwhile, his daughter Elisa grew into a strong Christian.

Almost all the people we have ministered to in the past seventeen years have not at first been willing to accept the authority and inspiration of the Scriptures. Nonetheless, only rarely have I had to discuss the subject, whether among non-Christians or with those we have brought to Christ. About the only useful information we have had to supply has been of a historical nature, the origins of the Bible, how the Scriptures came into existence, and when they were written.[1]

Since the Bible is authoritative, it assumes its rightful place as the new Christian is exposed to it. Gradually, unconsciously, he acknowledges its supremacy. This happens because the Bible is truth. The Bible brings light and truth to bear on the issues it addresses. When it considers man, life, society, and the world, its words ring true.

But the Scriptures go one step further. They uncover the fallacies and inconsistencies in our personal philosophies. "The word of God is living and active. Sharper than any double-edged sword, it penetrates even to dividing soul and spirit, joints and marrow; the thoughts and attitudes of the heart" (Hebrews 4:12).

What else can the non-Christian do when confronted by the living, mind-revealing and prophetic capacities of the Scriptures, but concede they are indeed authoritative? He will either submit to Christ, or admit he's just not willing for him to rule in his life.

WHERE TO BEGIN

What is the starting point? Where do we begin if we are to bring about this kind of response? The answer to this question depends entirely on the hearer's starting point. Where is he in his understanding? What does he accept? What does he know?

Whatever the case, the entire Christian message, and the entire Christian life for that matter, can be summarized with two questions. Our aim is to begin studying the Scriptures with a person at whatever point we find him in relation to these two questions. They were the questions Paul asked Jesus when he was struck down by a vision on the road to Damascus."Who are you, Lord?" and, "What shall I do, Lord?" (Acts 22:8,10).

Put another way, the two questions are, Who is Jesus? and, What does he want of me?

WHO IS JESUS?

The Bible builds its case on one historical figure, Jesus of Nazareth. He said, "If you really knew me, you would know my Father as well. From now on, you do know him and have seen him. . . . Anyone who has seen me has seen the Father" (John 14:7,9).

The basic affirmation of Christianity is that God is knowable because he has taken the initiative to bridge the gap between himself and man. This is critical because if it was not true, man would be left to make his own way to God with only his five frail senses to go on. He would get nowhere. In short, either Jesus was God, or God is unknowable. In that case we would all be lost in a sea of relativism.

According to the Scriptures, God has revealed himself in various ways throughout history, consummating the process in Jesus Christ. "In the past God spoke . . . through the prophets at many times and in various ways, but in these last days he has spoken to us by his Son. . . . The Son is the radiance of God's glory and *the exact representation of his being*" (Hebrews 1:1-3).

"The exact representation of his being." You can't believe God exists? Then who was Jesus? What about the justice of God —do you have problems with it too? Then look at Jesus. What was his sense of justice like? What about the problem of evil in the world? How did Jesus deal with evil? Is the Bible the inspired word of God? What did Jesus say about it?

Until we settle this basic question regarding the person of Jesus, we cannot speak conclusively to any other particulars. But when we arrive at the conclusion that Jesus is God, we discover that many of our other questions, that once seemed so insoluble, suddenly become either redundant or easily understood.

The Bible brings people to this conclusion about Jesus. The apostle John said his gospel was written "that you may believe that Jesus is the Christ, the Son of God, and that by believing you may have life in his name" (John 20:31).

Jesus took the unbelieving Jews to task for missing the point as to the basic intent of the Scriptures. He told them they diligently studied the Scriptures "because you think that by them you possess eternal life." But, he added, the intended purpose of the Scriptures is to "testify about me" (John 5:39).

So the first function of the Scriptures in leading a person to conversion is to answer, Who is Jesus? As we answer this question, the next one grows in importance.

WHAT DOES JESUS WANT OF ME?

Obviously, if the non-Christian draws any conclusion about Jesus other than that he is God, this second question is irrelevant. But if the conclusion is that he is who he claimed to be, every other concern in life is eclipsed by this question: What does he want of me?

If the Incarnation is true, if God actually became man, this fact must be of utmost significance to every man on earth. Consequently we must ask, What do you want of me?

For the non-Christian the answer is narrowed down to a single word: Believe.

On one occasion the multitude that followed Jesus asked a question very similar to the one we are discussing here: "What must we do to do the works God requires?" Jesus answered, "The work of God is this: to believe in the one He has sent" (John 6:28-29).

I'll never forget the day I understood the answer to this first question, Who is Jesus? The only logical response I could think of was to put the answer to the second question into action immediately. I acquired a notebook and spent weeks combing the Gospels for every command I could find. With two-thirds of the notebook filled, I despaired. I realized I could neither live up to it all, nor even keep track of it. I hadn't understood the dynamic nature of my subject matter. The Bible is a living book which speaks to life as we live it. The Bible comes alive through the promptings of the Holy Spirit according to our individual needs.

The fact is, we never outgrow either of these two questions. Continued progress in the Christian life comes as a result of further insight into Jesus Christ. Who is he, and what does he want me to do, are the first questions for every occasion in life. They are also the primary questions we ask as we daily read the Scriptures.

SUMMARY

God's means of communicating with unreconciled men and women are the Holy Spirit, the Scriptures, and the Christian. Each has a specific function. The Christian testifies to what he has seen and heard (See I John 1:1-3). He brings the non-Christian into contact with the Scriptures. Then the Holy Spirit does the convincing. It is through the "living and active" word of God (Hebrews 4:12) that an individual is born again.

It is important to keep this division of labor clear in our minds. For us to attempt to do the work of the Holy Spirit, or that of the Scriptures is futile. If a person is convinced by the Spirit of God, and spiritually reborn through the word of God, we can be confident of the kind of new life that has been created. It will bear fruit. As for us, we have had the privilege of making the introductions.

Footnotes:
1. F.F. Bruce's *The New Testament Documents: Are They Reliable?* (Downers Grove, Illinois: Inter-Varsity Press, 1959) supplies this kind of information, for example.

TWENTY-ONE

THE EXAMPLE OF ABRAHAO

You can't answer my questions

GOD ALLOWS A certain division of labor in the ministry of reconciliation. Christians, individually and collectively, bear witness by their life and word. They bring the non-Christian within hearing range of the Scriptures. The Scriptures reveal the truth and testify of Christ. The Holy Spirit convicts, draws the person to repentance, and gives life.

Now, how does all this take place? And more specifically, how should we proceed in order to make the most of all these resources in our evangelism?

Abrahao was an agricultural student at the University of Parana in Brazil. His purpose for being in school was not as much to get an education as it was to stimulate political unrest. He was a Communist. It happened that his roommate in the student boarding house where he lived was a new Christian. His name was Jark. Abrahao ridiculed Jark unmercifully until finally, in frustration, Jark invited Abrahao to one of our open studies. Abrahao had gotten what he wanted, the opportunity to cause one more disruption.

Abrahao sat in a corner of our living room where the study was taking place, apparently disinterested in everything that was being said. Suddenly, as the discussion was finally winding down, and everyone was becoming more interested in having coffee than in what was being said, Abrahao's hand went up. He asked the discussion leader a well-placed question. The leader paused to regroup his thoughts. As he did, Abrahao's hand went up again. He fired a second question. Now there were two questions to cope with. The leader became confused. The pause lengthened. Abrahao moved in with two or three more questions, one on top of the other. Finally, as the leader sat struggling with his confusion, Abrahao said, "See, you don't know what you're talking about. You can't answer my questions."

In the following weeks, Abrahao never missed a meeting. He did his best to create as much confusion as possible. I entertained the idea of asking him not to attend any more discussions, but I decided to make one last attempt to get through to him.

After our next study, as Abrahao and I were chatting, I asked him, "Abrahao, what kind of odds will you give me?"

He asked what I meant. I went on, "What kind of odds will you give me that I am right and that you are wrong—that God does exist?"

He laughed and replied, "None!"

Then I said, "Do you mean to tell me you have examined all known knowledge and have researched all unknown knowledge, and that you have scoured the universe, and now you stand before me saying, 'Relax, there is no God'?"

He replied, "I wouldn't say that."

I said, "Then you have to admit there is a possibility that I am right and you are wrong."

He conceded. I then pressed him: "What odds do you give me? Twenty percent?"

He said, "No."

I bargained for fifteen, ten, and finally said, "You must at least give me five percent."

He asked me what I was getting at. I replied, "If I'm right and you are wrong, you're dead. And since there is that possibility, the only rational thing for you to do is to check it out to see which of us is right."

He asked, "How do I do that?"

I replied, "Go to the original sources. Anyone doing serious research by-passes the secondary sources (what other people have said about a subject) and examines the original data."

He asked, "What are the original sources?"

I said, "The Bible."

He said, "I don't believe the Bible."

I said, "That gives you an advantage over me. The Bible is the only original source we Christians possess. If you can disprove the Bible, you win."

He asked, "What are you proposing?"

I explained, "The Bible is a thick book with fine print. You don't read it like any other book—from start to finish—because it is really a library of sixty-six volumes. You are going to need help in knowing which book to pull off the shelf first. My offer is to show you where to look and to help you understand what it says."

Abrahao accepted my offer and we set a date for our first meeting.

I introduced him to the Gospel of John. We started by my asking him to read the first three verses: "In the beginning was the Word, and the Word was with God, and the Word was God. He was with God in the beginning. Through him all things were made; without him nothing was made that has been made" (John 1:1-3).

I asked Abrahao if he understood what was being said. He didn't. I asked him, "What does the word *Word* refer to?"

He didn't know, so I referred him to verse 14: "The Word became flesh and lived for a while among us."

With a little help he realized the passage was talking about

Jesus Christ. When he understood that the Bible claimed Jesus was eternal and that he had created all things, he was ready to fight. I defused his arguments by saying, "I'm not asking you to believe or to agree with what is written here. I just want to make sure you understand what it says. Do you?"

He replied, "Yes, but—"

I said, "Good, let's go on to the next paragraph."

As we worked our way through the next passages over the following weeks, Abrahao didn't appear to budge an inch. He assigned every claim about Christ to legends or exaggerated accounts. I stuck to the single objective of helping him understand what the Bible was saying about who Jesus was. Thus, in spite of his rebellion, our meetings, though always electric, were debate-free.

Meanwhile, my friends and I prayed that the Holy Spirit would accomplish his work of persuasion.

After a few months I began to spot signs of change. Abrahao quit disagreeing with the Scriptures. He began to see the relationships between one passage and another. He gradually changed from a generally negative person to being positive. He volunteered to spend his summer vacation working on a government-sponsored project for the poor. When the summer was over, he returned as an old friend, no longer as an adversary. Without a word we went back to studying the Gospel of John.

Finally, I could contain my curiosity no longer. He was so changed! As we sat down to study John 13, I said, "Okay, Abrahao, what's happened?"

He replied, "Yeah, it's true."

"What's true?"

"Jesus is God."

"So?" I pressed him.

"Well, I guess I'm a Christian now. But," he went on, "I need to tell you one thing. I'm politically active, and I've taken a position which is against our government. I'm also anti-American. My friends criticize me for seeing you."

I said, "Go on."

He said, "That's it. I just thought you should know."

"Do you think it makes any difference with me?"

"No."

Then I said, "I'd like to show you a verse." It happened to be in the chapter we were about to study. We turned to John 13:13: "You call me 'Teacher' and 'Lord,' and rightly so, for that is what I am."

I asked Abrahao, "What does it mean if Jesus is our teacher?"

His reply was perfect. "It means what we think and believe must come from him. We refer our ideas back to him."

"Do you accept that?"

"Yes."

"What does it mean for Jesus to be Lord?"

Again his reply was excellent. "It means he's the boss."

"Do you accept that?"

He said yes.

We never did discuss politics or economics. Abrahao and I were now under the same teacher and under the same authority—Jesus Christ. Both of us were responding to the same call: "Be worthy citizens of the kingdom."

What is the lesson from this illustration?

Our job is to help a person *understand* the Scriptures. The burden of proof is not on us, but on them. The responsibility to convince lies with the Holy Spirit, not with me. I am responsible to be faithful to that person by maintaining his exposure to the word of God until a final decision is made, for or against.

I have a Christian friend who is one of those beautiful people who attracts every person he meets. He always seems to say the right thing at the right time. He witnesses with ease wherever he goes, and leaves people hungry for more. When we first became friends years ago I thought, Here is one person who is going to make an impact.

It never materialized. He's beautiful like a butterfly, but you can never count on a butterfly to land on the same flower twice. Bringing a secularized person to Christ requires perseverance and tenacity. It means establishing and maintaining a relationship as he goes through the throes of resistance. At times, it is only that relationship that holds the non-Christian from rejecting the Holy Spirit and running away.

Obviously this is costly. It costs hours as well as emotional and spiritual energy. If we are not convinced of the eternal worth of the individual, we'll never do it.

TWENTY-TWO

SUGGESTIONS FOR APPLICATION
How to get involved

THIS BOOK'S MAJOR emphasis is that there are two modes of evangelism in the New Testament: proclamation and affirmation. Proclamation is essential, with the primary function of establishing a beachhead. Some Christians have special abilities in the area of proclamation, which should be used to the fullest extent. But proclamation is limited in its effectiveness to the relative few who have been previously prepared to listen receptively to the Christian gospel.

Affirmation is necessary if we are to go beyond the initial task of reaching the prepared. Understanding this will make a significant difference in our concept of evangelism. Everyone in the body of Christ can be involved in affirmation evangelism. Evangelism can be a normal and spontaneous aspect of our lives. Affirmation is not limited to those with highly developed communication skills. If we recognize the primary responsibility of the Holy Spirit and the function of the body of Christ in affirmation evangelism, there will be little room for fear, guilt, frustration, or a sense of personal failure.

How can we be personally involved in affirmation evangelism? To answer I would like to review the major emphases of the book, giving guidelines and suggestions for application. This is not a detailed manual, but a list of practical helps for you to consider and apply.

STEP ONE:

RECOGNIZE THERE IS A NEEDY, UNREACHED WORLD OUT THERE

We need to recognize the problem on a broad scale. There are billions of people in the world who are entirely beyond the scope of our present evangelistic efforts. More important initially is the problem on the individual level. We are all surrounded by people with whom we have no contact, who are mentally and emotionally worlds apart from us. Are there people within your sphere of influence whom you are not influencing with the gospel? Will they ever be reached by your usual methods? Is it your responsibility to go to them? In all probability you will recognize many people within your own neighborhood and among your own relatives, and entire groups of people within your own city who are not likely to respond to what you're doing now.

STEP TWO:

UNDERSTAND THE LIMITS OF PROCLAMATION

Proclamation has its applications as well as its limitations. Remember that Paul, in his use of proclamation, sought out those who had a religious heritage—those who were prepared. As you think about people around you, how many of them would go to a public place with you to hear the gospel? Or how many would understand and accept what they heard? How many could make an intelligent response to even the best door-to-door presentation of the gospel?

Redoubling our efforts in proclamation will reach more prepared people. This is a worthwhile objective, but we need to go further.

You may have a special ability for proclamation. Your witnessing is producing results. God has given you sufficient contact with people whom he has prepared for your witness. You are satisfied and fulfilled in the direction you are going.

You may have experienced satisfaction in evangelism but realize there are many within your sphere of influence who are not responding to your verbal witness. You feel the need to reach out even further.

Or you may be experiencing some frustration concerning evangelism. You have been challenged all of your Christian life in regard to your obligation to witness, but feel you don't have the ability. In this area of life you feel defeated.

You may be one of the few who are completely frustrated. God has placed you in a situation where there are virtually no prepared people. Your training and experience in evangelism have been limited to proclamation and it simply doesn't work. Many missionaries are in this position.

STEP THREE:
GET INVOLVED IN AFFIRMATION EVANGELISM

1. *Find a balance to the reaping mentality.* Recognize that evangelism is a process. Planting, watering, and cultivating all precede reaping the harvest. Be willing and satisfied to contribute at any stage of the process. For the unprepared, it is a long road into the kingdom of God. Seek to help those you know to take their next step, rather than forcing a superficial conversion.

2. *Build your life on the foundation of God's word.* We have talked about modeling a viable option, of establishing congruence in our lives, and of living a good testimony. Our lives should be attractive to those around us, offering a real option. Our entire value system, that is our morality and philosophy of life, should agree with the Scriptures. Our good testimony should not be a legalistic caricature, but a demonstration of grace.

Of course, perfection in this is impossible to achieve. But if we are making an honest effort to be conformed to the image of Christ, we will stand in marked contrast to the world around us. It is not necessary or even desirable to project a perfect image. Paul recognized this: "Not that I have already attained all this, or I have already been made perfect" (Philippians 3:12). We need to demonstrate not perfection, but the grace of God. Faith, in spite of failures, is what communicates to those around us. If we project ourselves as pious and perfect, others will only be discouraged. We are imperfect, but redeemed.

3. *Face the problems of isolation, fear, and adaptation.* If your separation from the world around you has become isolation, *change your lifestyle.* Jesus was the friend of publicans and sinners. We must accept people as they are. Be realistic about people and don't expect too much. They are not Christians, and they will probably act accordingly. Don't come across as a reformer.

Acceptance does not mean approval. The contrast between your values and theirs will become conspicuous. Be sure this contrast is based on moral and scriptural matters, not on trivial and optional things. It is our responsibility to adapt to them unless absolute moral issues are involved. Make them feel comfortable around you. Be "all things to all men." Remember that sanctification is a matter of the heart, not surroundings.

Avoid judging, preaching, condemning, or moralizing. "No, thank you" is definitely preferable to "I don't smoke because I'm a Christian and the Bible says—" Prayer before lunch that embarrasses your guest is not necessarily a good testimony! Demonstrate grace, not legalism. Be sensitive as to how your actions will affect the other person.

Love people as they are and as individuals, not as targets for evangelism. Love. Accept. Adapt. Be a friend.

We've talked about changing our attitudes. We will also need to change our priorities. Building good relationships with people involves time. Most Christians are incredibly busy. A radical adjustment in our schedules is essential. One pastor I know told his people that one meeting in church each week was enough, otherwise they would rob prime time from being with non-Christians. If your neighbor wants to go out for a pizza and you can't find time this week, he won't be calling you next week! An important word in building relationships with people is *availability*.

4. *Seek out a few like-minded people.* Few of us can accomplish anything alone. We need encouragement. We need to pray together, to sharpen one another's vision and to function effectively as the body. In the process of affirmation evangelism, there will be times when it is necessary to expose non-Christians to other Christians besides yourself. An institution won't serve that purpose well for secularized people. This exposure to other Christians serves several purposes. It reinforces your witness by adding credibility. It broadens the potential for direct influence, since all of us do not have the same capacity for verbalization. Someone else in the group may be better equipped to communicate in a given situation. This makes affirmation a group effort. Everyone contributing to the group becomes involved in the process of evangelism. Gifts are exercised within the group, where each individual reinforces the other. Pool your resources. Take an inventory of what each member can do.

5. *Prepare yourself to verbalize the gospel.* While a formal presentation of the gospel produces direct results among the prepared, verbalization is an essential ingredient in the process of affirmation. It will occur on various levels:

> The casual references to Christ's involvement in our lives; his influence on our personal value system
> The personal witness or testimony of how we met Christ
> The clear presentation of the gospel that synthesizes God's plan of reconciliation
> The teaching of the Scriptures for the purpose of evangelism, on the individual or small group level

Look back over this list. Where do you feel most deficient? Which of these would you really like to master? What could you do to achieve this? Who do you know that could help you? What books or materials could help?

The aim is to share our faith *naturally*. That takes preparation—and experience., Get into it. When you find you're in over your head, get someone with more experience to help you. Observe how that person does it and soon you'll be able to do as well.

6. *Begin to take initiatives in establishing relationships.* Just to become aware of the people around us and begin to greet them is a big step. Be the first to say, "Hello." Be friendly.

Seek rapport. Look for the common ground. Rapport occurs when two people share common interests and/or needs. This will cost you time and privacy, but how will others see God's grace in us if we keep our distance?

Love! God's love for man is unconditional. His love is expressed through us as we commit ourselves to seeking the good of another, regardless of his response to us (see 1 John 3:16-18). There is an obvious link between loving and serving. If you answer the question, In what way can I serve this person?, you will have answered the question, How can I love him?

Reinforce and supplement your newly-made relationships by drawing some of your like-minded Christian friends into them. This could mean anything from a backyard barbecue to a jazz concert to a Bible study group.

7. *Single out and pray for individuals.* "When he saw the crowds . . . harrassed and helpless . . . He said to his disciples . . . 'Ask the Lord of the harvest, therefore, to send out workers'" (Matthew 9:36-38). So you have no burden for the lost? Stop, and observe those around you! Then pray. Ask God to do something about what you see. Volunteer your services to him and see what happens! First he will probably call certain individuals to your attention. He means for you to pray for them. Be faithful. Pray your way through every step of the process, from establishing the first rapport, to opening the door to the message, to the Holy Spirit's convicting them of sin, righteousness, and judgment.

Persist in prayer (see Luke 11:9-10). George Mueller wrote, "The great point is to never give up until that answer comes. I have been praying every day for 52 years for two men, sons of a friend of my youth. They are not converted yet, but they will be! . . . The great fault of the children of God is that they do not continue in prayer—they do not go on praying; they do not persevere. If they desire anything for God's glory, they should pray until they get it."[1]

One of these men became a Christian at George Mueller's funeral, the other some years later.

8. *Invite your friends to study the Scriptures with you.* You have been transparent from the start of your relationship about the source of your lifestyle. Your friends know it's the Bible. As it's reality and practicality become apparent, their curiosity and interest will grow. Often as a result of your prayers and the love you have shown, a person will respond to your invitation with an eagerness that will reveal they have been *waiting for you to get around to inviting them.*

Be candid and clear in your invitation. Remember, you are not out to extract an immediate decision, but to give them the opportunity to get a first-hand look at the word of God and the Son of God.

Bible studies can be held with an individual, with a few couples, or in small groups. If you don't feel comfortable leading a study yourself, team up with someone who can do it. But if you can possibly do it yourself, do it. Good study aids and materials are available. Or, just work your way through the book of John or Romans.

9. *Rely on the Holy Spirit.* Give him time to work. Follow his timing, not your own. Your job is to make the message of the Scriptures clear. Let him take it from there.

Be alert to the circumstances that affect a person's life as he gets into the Scriptures. Often things go from bad to worse, a sign that he is struggling with his basic rebellion against God. Or, a crisis will occur that is beyond his control. Be encouraged! God uses such crises to awaken us to our needs. Be there as a friend when those things happen. The security of your acceptance, love, and friendship is usually more important than your counsel or advice during such times.

10. *Stick with them.* Persevere. The easiest part of an evangelistic Bible study is the actual study itself. The bigger challenge is to generate the desire to attend and to sustain the interest over the long haul. You won't get far if your only contact is during your discussions. Make sure you also have some sort of informal interchange between encounters. It doesn't take much. In fact, be careful not to overdo it. "Seldom set foot in your neighbor's house—too much of you, and he will hate you" (Proverbs 25:17). A ten-minute visit is enough time to gather some feedback and to verify the time and place of your next meeting. But it is essential. And it may be such informal moments which open the way for deeper conversations.

CONCLUSION

In 1937 the first edition of *Think and Grow Rich* by Napoleon Hill was published. It was the product of twenty years of research done at the prompting of Andrew Carnegie. As part of his research, Napoleon Hill interviewed hundreds of America's most successful entrepreneurs; men like King Gillette, Henry Ford, William Wrigley, Jr., Thomas Edison, and John D. Rockefeller. He was looking for the common denominators among these men, the characteristics they shared that explained their success. Once he identified, interpreted, and organized these qualities, Mr. Hill presented them as a philosophy for financial success. Since 1937, *Think and Grow Rich* has sold more than forty-two editions—a testimony of its popularity and influence on American society. But I thought the book was diabolical.

Essentially, Mr. Hill's conclusion is that if you wish to become wealthy, you must develop an obsession for money. You must meditate on it, plan for it, and sacrifice anything in order to get it. Money must become the top priority in your value system.

But I agree with Mr. Hill's basic observation: Today's obsessions become tomorrow's realities. "Above all else, guard your heart, for it is the wellspring of life" (Proverbs 4:23).

What are your obsessions? Are they the same as God's? What is God doing? He is putting all things right, reconciling everyone to himself (see Colossians 1:15-20).

Evangelizing lost, secularized people—this book's subject—is central to what is on God's heart. It is a worthy obsession. Make it yours.

Footnotes:

1. George Mueller, *George Mueller Man of Faith* (a reprint of *An Hour With George Mueller The Man of Faith to Whom God Gave Millions,* published by Warren Myers, 12 Siglap Close, Singapore 15), page 9.